50 FINDS
FROM YORKSHIRE
Objects from the Portable
Antiquities Scheme

Amy Downes and Rebecca Griffiths

AMBERLEY

About the Authors

Amy Downes

Originally from Somerset, Amy Downes gained a first class degree in archaeology from the University of York and has stayed in Yorkshire ever since. She worked at the Yorkshire Museum and Malton Museum before joining the Portable Antiquities Scheme in 2006 as Finds Liaison Officer for South and West Yorkshire. She has recorded over 10,000 archaeological objects on the PAS database. Amy enjoys identifying medieval coins, and is slowly learning to love flint tools.

Rebecca Griffiths

While studying archaeology at the University of York, Rebecca Griffiths began volunteering with the Portable Antiquities Scheme. This inspired a keen interest in small finds and, following her graduation in 2009, she gained an internship with the PAS. Rebecca, a native of York, was appointed Finds Liaison Officer for North and East Yorkshire in 2011 and has also recorded over 10,000 finds. She enjoys working with artefacts from all periods of history, though she has a particular interest in the coinage of the Roman Empire.

York Museums Trust

First published 2016

Amberley Publishing
The Hill, Stroud
Gloucestershire, GL5 4EP

www.amberley-books.com

Copyright © Amy Downes and Rebecca Griffiths, 2016

The right of Amy Downes and Rebecca Griffiths to be identified as the Authors of this work has been asserted in accordance with the Copyrights, Designs and Patents Act 1988.

ISBN 978 1 4456 6146 9 (print)
ISBN 978 1 4456 6147 6 (ebook)

British Library Cataloguing in Publication Data.
A catalogue record for this book is available from the British Library.

Typeset in 10pt on 13pt Celeste.
Typesetting by Amberley Publishing.
Printed in the UK.

Contents

Acknowledgements

This book is the result of twenty years of the Portable Antiquities Scheme (PAS) recording finds in Yorkshire. The current Finds Liaison Officers have been in post for ten years (Amy) and six years (Rebecca), but we are indebted to the previous post-holders who established the scheme in Yorkshire, and who forged the initial links with local finders and museums.

We are also grateful to all our current and previous colleagues at the PAS for their hard work and dedication, for their support, and for their willingness to share their knowledge and expertise. Both of us have also been aided over the years by fantastic interns, students and volunteers, many of whom have been giving up their time for the PAS for many years.

We would like to thank our husbands and families for their patience, forbearance and proof-reading, as well as for their practical support with babysitting, IT assistance and graphic-design skills. We are also very grateful that our cats did not delete anything massively important while attempting to snooze on our keyboards. Arthur deserves special mention for his patience while mummy worked every weekend, as does Eliza, for timing her unexpectedly early birth impeccably between submitting the manuscript and receiving the proofs.

Colleagues in our host and partner organisations have also been tremendously helpful. We'd particularly like to thank the Yorkshire Museum's Andrew Woods and Adam Parker for sharing their expertise and proof-reading skills, Paula Gentil at Hull & East Riding Museum for her constant support and advice, Ian Sanderson and the staff at the West Yorkshire Archaeology Advisory Service for their generous assistance, and the South Yorkshire Archaeology Service for their guidance. Thanks are also given to all the curators and staff of South and West Yorkshire's nine museum services who kindly allowed us access to their collections: Barnsley Museums, Bradford Museums and Galleries, Calderdale MBC Museums, Doncaster MBC Museums and Galleries, Kirklees Council's Museums, Galleries and History Team, Leeds Museums and Galleries, Rotherham MBC Museums and Galleries, Museums Sheffield and Wakefield Council's Museums Team.

Unless otherwise stated, images are courtesy of the Portable Antiquities Scheme. Every attempt has been made to seek permission for copyrighted material used in this book. However, if we have inadvertently used copyrighted material without permission or acknowledgement, we apologise and will make the necessary correction at the first opportunity.

Finally, we owe a huge debt of gratitude to the finders who volunteer their artefacts for recording with the PAS and allow us to hold history in our hands. Without them, this book would not have been possible.

Foreword

The places in which we live and work have a long past, but one that is not always obvious in the landscape around us. This is a forgotten past. Most of us know little about the people who once lived in our communities fifty years ago, let alone 500, or even 5,000 years past. Like us, they lived, played and worked here, in this place, but we know almost nothing of them.

History books tell us about royalty, great lords and important churchmen, but most others are forgotten by time. The only evidence for many of these people is the objects that they left behind; sometimes buried on purpose, but more often lost by chance. Sometimes, through archaeological fieldwork, we can place these objects in a context that allows us to better understand the past, but nowadays excavation is mostly development led and so only takes place when a new building, road or service pipe is being constructed.

A unique way of understanding the past is through the finds recorded through the Portable Antiquities Scheme of which those chosen here by Amy Downes (South & West Yorkshire Finds Liaison Officer) and Rebecca Griffiths (North & East Yorkshire Finds Liaison Officer) are just fifty of over 57,000 from Yorkshire on its database (www.finds.org.uk). These finds are all discovered by the public, most by metal-detector users, searching in places archaeologists are unlikely to go or otherwise excavate. As such, they provide important clues of underlying archaeology that (once recorded) help archaeologists understand our past – a past of the people, found by the people.

Some of these finds are truly magnificent, others less imposing. Yet, like pieces in a jigsaw puzzle they are often meaningless alone, but once placed together paint a picture. These finds therefore allow us to understand the story of people who once lived here, in Yorkshire.

Dr Michael Lewis
Head of Portable Antiquities & Treasure
British Museum

Introduction

Portable Antiquities Scheme

www.finds.org.uk

Every year thousands of archaeological objects are found by members of the public. When properly recorded, these objects can contribute significantly to our understanding of the country's history. These discoveries are usually unearthed in rural areas where traditional archaeological investigation occurs less frequently. As such, they can tell us about ordinary people, as well as the big events that shaped the region.

A recently discovered medieval penny. (Peter Smith)

The British Museum's Portable Antiquities Scheme (PAS) was established to encourage the voluntary recording of archaeological objects, in order to advance our knowledge of the past. It achieves this through its network of Finds Liaison Officers (FLOs), hosted in offices around the country, who liaise with finders to ensure a digital record of archaeological finds is made. These records are publicly accessible through the PAS's online database, which is a virtual museum containing over one million objects.

FLOs work closely with coroners to administer the Treasure Act 1996, which replaced the medieval Treasure Trove law. Under the Act, the term 'Treasure' encompasses objects that contain at least 10 per cent precious metal and that are at least 300 years old, as well as hoards and some prehistoric objects. For more information, see the Treasure Act 1996 or contact your local FLO. The reporting of items of potential Treasure is mandatory and gives museums the opportunity to acquire artefacts for the benefit of the nation. Several of the fifty finds in this book were acquired in this way.

Many of the finds recorded with the PAS are discovered by metal-detector users. The PAS advocates best practice and encourages finders to adhere to the Code of Practice for Responsible Metal Detecting. The growth of metal detecting and formal reporting offered by the PAS has made much more material available for study, which helps with the interpretation of objects that were previously unique or where only a handful were known.

Responsible metal detecting generates many of the finds recorded by the PAS. (Peter Smith)

The PAS also engages local communities with their heritage, encouraging them to enhance the history of their area and, on a larger scale, the country. The resulting records represent a substantial contribution to archaeological knowledge, which aids researchers at all levels. The quantity and quality of material recorded by the PAS is guiding professional archaeologists and is allowing standard reference texts to be rewritten by feeding in new information.

The Yorkshire landscape has evolved over thousands of years, influenced by geology, climate and human activity. It is huge and varied, comprising dramatic and contrasting landscapes from the coastline of the east, the rolling chalklands of the Wolds, the sweeping Dales and foreboding Pennines, to the largely agricultural landscapes of the Vales of York, Pickering and Mowbray. These diverse settings have, in part, determined the nature of the towns and cities set within them. These areas support a wide range of land uses, including arable, pasture, and woodland, with a variety of natural and historic features. Yorkshire's archaeological heritage is equally rich, with fascinating sites such as Duggleby Howe, prehistoric art on Ilkley Moor, Aldborough Roman Villa and Conisbrough Castle coming together to tell its story. The work of the PAS has added to our understanding of the region, highlighting newly discovered areas of ancient activity and regionally specific artefact types, some of which are discussed in this book.

Yorkshire has two FLOs. The North and East Yorkshire post was established in 1996 and is based at the Yorkshire Museum, while the FLO post for South and West Yorkshire, established in 2004, is based at the West Yorkshire Archaeology Advisory Service. Over

The Yorkshire Dales near Ingleborough. (Chris Downes)

A prehistoric cup-and-ring marked stone on Ilkley Moor. (Ian Downes)

North and East Yorkshire FLO Rebecca Griffiths discussing a Roman brooch with the finder.

57,000 objects have been recorded from the region, including many exceptional and significant discoveries.

Both FLOs regularly attend meetings of metal-detecting groups in their areas and hold Finds Days in partner museums. Outreach events, such as talks to local groups and societies, enable the FLOs to promote the scheme as a research and educational tool, and speaking at conferences facilitates the sharing of information gathered through recorded finds.

50 Finds from Yorkshire highlights some of the PAS's most interesting discoveries and explores how they weave into the narrative of the past, helping to reshape our understanding of one of the most significant counties of Britain. The full record of each featured object is publicly accessible through the PAS database at www.finds.org.uk, and can be viewed by entering the unique reference code (YORYM-123456, for example) into the search bar.

South and West Yorkshire FLO Amy Downes admiring Roman pottery brought in for recording.

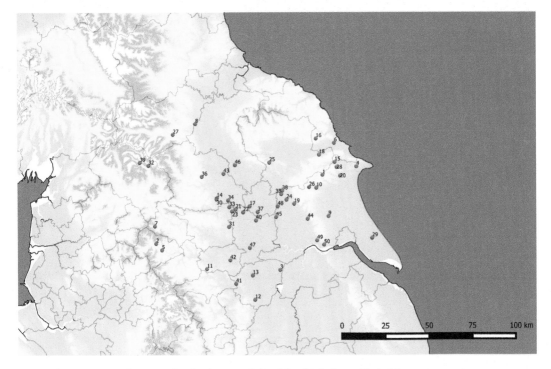

Above: A map showing the findspots of the fifty finds from Yorkshire.

Below: A heat map showing all finds recorded by the PAS from Yorkshire, alongside the fifty finds in this book.

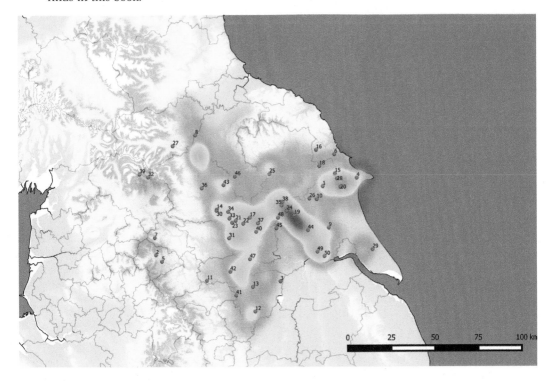

Chapter 1
Prehistory

Roseberry Topping, North Yorkshire, is an iconic natural monument at the heart of a prehistoric landscape. (Graeme and Emma Watson)

The prehistoric period begins with the emergence of the human species around five million years ago, and ends with the arrival of the Romans and the advent of the written word. It encompasses three seemingly distinct periods: the Stone Age, Bronze Age and Iron Age.

In reality, this period is far more complex, and no clear moment of change exists from one age to the next. New technologies were adopted at different times in various parts of the country. The Stone Age alone covers over 800,000 years and is further sub-divided into the Palaeolithic, Mesolithic and Neolithic periods.

Palaeolithic (c. 500,000–10,000 BC)

During the Palaeolithic (Early Stone Age), northern parts of Britain, including Yorkshire, were frequently covered with glaciers, making continuous habitation impossible. During warmer periods both Neanderthals and early *Homo sapiens* visited, leaving evidence in the form of tools, but subsequent glacial action wiped the landscape clean. Accordingly, very few Palaeolithic artefacts are found in Yorkshire.

1. Flint hand axe (YORYM-818451)
Palaeolithic, *c.* 500,000–*c.* 200,000 BC
Discovered in 2012 in Cottam, East Riding.

Only seven Palaeolithic objects have been recorded with the PAS from Yorkshire, including this flint hand axe. Mined from prehistory onwards, flint was used for the manufacture of the oldest known tools. Over time, as plankton and sponges died and collected on the sea bed, a silica-rich layer formed, which was compressed into flint. Most of Yorkshire was intermittently covered by deep ice sheets at this time and, while some small nodules or pebbles were collected from local beaches or eroding boulder clay deposits, the majority of flint was drawn in from other areas by the movement of ice sheets.

Tools such as this hand axe were created by taking a flint nodule and striking small flakes off it until the desired shape was achieved, a process known as 'knapping'. They were used for a variety of purposes, such as butchery, digging, harvesting plants and chopping wood.

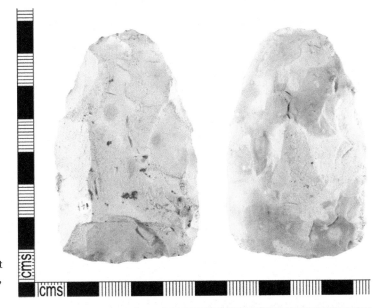

YORYM-818451: A flint hand axe from Cottam, East Riding.

Flint being knapped using a hard hammer stone. (C. Hayward Trevarthen)

13

Mesolithic (c. 10,000–4000 BC)

The last ice age came to an end around 10,000 years ago, marking the start of the Mesolithic (Middle Stone Age). Britain was still connected to mainland Europe and the climate was initially sub-arctic, supporting animals such as mammoths and woolly rhinoceroses. As the climate improved, rich vegetation thrived and sustained a population of hunter-gatherer communities. By 5000 BC, rising sea levels had separated Britain from the Continent.

The earliest evidence for settlement in Yorkshire comes from Star Carr in the Vale of Pickering, which is regarded as the most important Mesolithic site in Great Britain. Located on the banks of the prehistoric Lake Flixton, waterlogged conditions allowed exceptional preservation of organic remains, meaning that many different types of artefact survive. Exciting finds from the site include Britain's oldest known structure, red-deer skull headdresses, hundreds of projectile points made from red-deer antler, and an engraved shale pendant bearing the earliest known Mesolithic art in Britain.

The presence of lasting structures, such as a house and jetty at Star Carr, suggest long-term occupation, but Mesolithic people are thought to have been highly mobile, moving about the landscape in small groups. Deepcar, near Sheffield, is a more typical temporary Mesolithic camp; it gives its name to specific types of flint tools that were first discovered there.

A life-sized model of a woolly mammoth, displayed in the Hull and East Riding Museum. (Hull and East Riding Museum, Hull Museums; accession number: 2008.64)

A unique, engraved shale pendant from Star Carr – the oldest Mesolithic art in Britain. (The POSTGLACIAL project; http://intarch.ac.uk/journal/issue40/8/index.html)

In the Mesolithic, a 'blade technology' developed in which long, thin pieces of flint were fashioned into tools. This new technology created small, portable objects, such as the characteristic Microlith, which accompanied the nomadic hunter-gatherer lifestyle. Small pieces of flint were carefully removed by applying controlled pressure (pressure-flaking) to shape the piece, leaving visible scars on the edges. Groups of these tiny flints would have been used together to form composite tools.

Microliths from Calderdale and Kirklees are uniquely smaller than those from other areas. This is probably because the flints from the West Yorkshire Pennines are eroding from sites of a specific date wherein very small tools were in fashion. It may be that archaeological layers of a similar date are not currently exposed in other parts of the country.

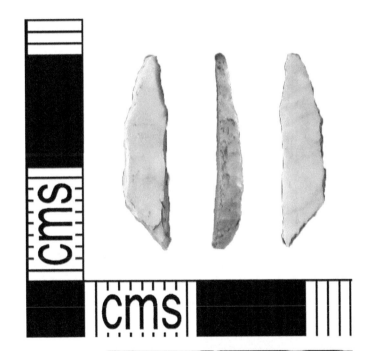

SWYOR-6E962B: A flint microlith from Hebdon Royd, Calderdale.

The technique of pressure-flaking involves removing flakes from a struck flint by pushing them off with a tool made of a softer material. Bone or antler were used in the Mesolithic and Neolithic periods, but copper (as illustrated here) was used for pressure-flaking in the Bronze Age. (C. Hayward Trevarthen)

Not all Mesolithic tools were extremely small. This adze is a wood-working tool that has been knapped from flint to produce a sharp cutting blade. It would have been hafted to a wood or antler handle for use. As there is no naturally occurring flint in South Yorkshire, either the raw material or the finished tool was imported, probably from the Yorkshire coast.

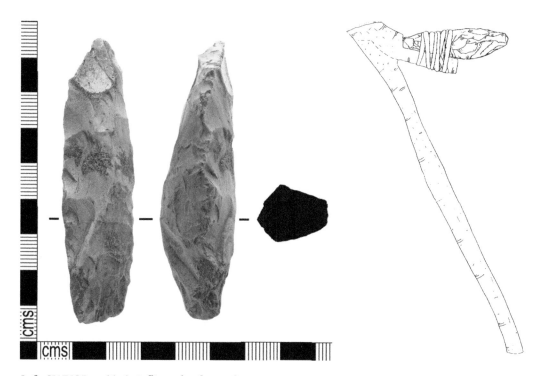

Left: SWYOR-536696: A flint adze from Thorn, Doncaster.

Right: A diagram showing how the flint adze could have been bound (hafted) to a wooden handle for use.

Neolithic (c. 4000–2350 BC)

The introduction of farming is widely regarded as one of the biggest advancements in human history, and marks the beginning of the Neolithic period. In response to an improving climate and the need for sustainable food sources, people became more settled, gradually adopting agriculture over 2,000 years. Farmers grew crops, kept animals, made pottery and were highly skilled at making stone implements, including axes that were used to clear forests.

New forms of flint tools developed, usually made from broad flakes rather than narrow blades. Permanent settlements and the first communal tombs, known as 'long barrows', were constructed, and society became more hierarchical. This greater social division is reflected in the development of monumental structures such as cairns and stone circles like the famous Stonehenge. In Yorkshire, the Thornborough Henges (a complex including three aligned henges with burial grounds and settlements) is the most significant ancient site between Stonehenge and Orkney.

Major Neolithic sites are also found on the Yorkshire Wolds, placing the region among the most important in the country. In particular, Rudston boasts four major ceremonial monuments and the Rudston Monolith, which is the tallest standing stone in Britain.

Left: A reconstruction drawing of a typical Neolithic farming scene. (Dominic Andrews)

Right: The Rudston Monolith stands at over 25 feet (7.5 metres) high. (Dr Kevin Leahy)

4. Polished stone axe head (YORYM-AoBo88)
Neolithic, *c.* 3500–2100 BC
Discovered in 2015 in Bridlington, East Riding.

This unfinished stone axe head demonstrates the evolution of tool types with the addition of polishing at the end of the shaping process. It is made of a grey-green sedimentary volcanic rock from the Great Langdale quarries in Cumbria, which was probably chosen for its colour and fineness.

Axe heads made of Langdale stone have been found throughout England and represent important evidence for the exchange of goods and materials in the Neolithic period.

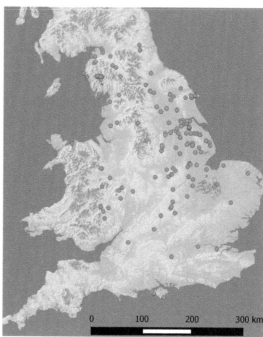

Above left: YORYM-AoBo88: A stone axe head from Bridlington, East Riding.

Above right: A map showing the distribution of Langdale axes recorded with the PAS.

Left: Great Langdale from Rossett Pike, from where stone was quarried in the Neolithic period to produce axes. (Mick Knapton – https://commons.wikimedia.org/wiki/File:Great_Langdale_from_Rossett_Pike.jpg)

Discovered on an allotment, this knife is a good example of the high level of workmanship that went into Neolithic tools. The blade is extremely thin, making it translucent, and most of the surface displays delicate working called scalar retouch. This has been done at a shallow angle to create a sharp cutting tool, which would have been hafted for use. The slight curve on the tool, and the uncertainty as to how much is missing, could mean that it is actually part of a sickle – a curved knife used for harvesting plants.

SWYOR-4A386D: A flint knife from Sowerby Bridge, Calderdale.

Bronze Age (*c.* 2350–800 BC)

The development of metalworking marks the beginning of the Bronze Age and was an important technological development, especially the ability to control fire. A large number of metalwork hoards, where groups of spearheads, axes and daggers were placed in the ground together, are found from this period, reflecting the importance of this newly tamed material.

Metal tools involved a huge investment of time, resources and energy, so flint and stone tools continued to be used and adapted. Copper tools were used to pressure-flake distinctive flint arrowheads, which are every bit as diagnostic of the British Bronze Age as metal tools.

The adoption of metal objects was gradual as people continued to farm, hunt, and clear forests. The early Bronze Age can be seen as a continuation of the Neolithic period, with prehistoric monumental landscapes such as the barrows, henge and cists at Ferrybridge originating in the Neolithic and continuing in use into the Bronze Age and beyond. From about 1500 BC, the landscape started to be divided up with stone rows, as people began to claim ownership of land and to feel the need to defend it.

Burials took place beneath circular mounds known as round barrows and were often accompanied by bronze artefacts and pottery. Most barrows are in prominent upland locations such as the Wolds, Moors and Pennines, and were often designed to be visible landscape features.

Left: A Bronze Age hoard from County Durham, containing axes and axe fragments, probably gathered together for re-melting and reuse. Many of the axes are Yorkshire type axes, which, as the name suggests, are common in Northern England (NCL-12C141/2008T483).

Below: A reconstruction drawing of the Ferrybridge prehistoric landscape, showing the large Neolithic henge (background) and smaller Bronze Age barrows (middle), as it appeared in the Iron Age farming landscape (foreground). (ASWYAS)

6. Flint barbed and tanged arrowhead (YORYM-B4DC69)
Bronze Age, c. 2000–1500 BC
Discovered in 2015 in Carlton Town, North Yorkshire.

A wide range of elaborate flint tools were produced during the Bronze Age, including a variety of arrowheads such as this distinctive barbed and tanged type, unearthed by a mole. These objects were made from various types of stone by striking flakes, which were then finely shaped using pressure-flaking.

These arrowheads are generally triangular, with two small notches chipped into the base to form the central tang and flanking barbs. The tang was used to secure the arrowhead to its shaft, and usually projects slightly below the ends of the barbs. The barbs prevented the arrow being dislodged as the animal bolted. If the arrow was removed, the barbs caused a vicious wound, ensuring the hunters did not have far to track their prey.

YORYM-B4DC69: A flint barbed and tanged arrowhead from Carlton Town, North Yorkshire.

7. Ceramic burial urns (SWYOR-C4F166, 2007 T388)
Bronze Age, c. 2150–1500 BC
Discovered in 2007 in Stanbury, Bradford, and acquired by Cliffe Castle Museum,
Keighley.

Though early Bronze Age people were buried in barrows, the later Bronze Age saw a shift to the rite of cremation. This group of three burial urns was discovered during garden landscaping work and, as soon as the top of the largest was uncovered, the finder reported it to the local museum, allowing professional archaeologists to excavate it.

The urns were buried in a single pit. The largest contained cremated human remains, accompanied by a stone battle-axe or macehead; a bone pin; a bone belt-fastener; and two partially melted pieces of copper alloy, interpreted as earrings.

The human remains are believed to be those of a young man. The objects placed with him suggest that he was someone special. The battle-axe is thought to be an object of power, so perhaps he was a warrior or tribal leader. The other two urns are smaller and probably contained offerings such as food for the afterlife.

An archaeologist from Archaeological Services: West Yorkshire Archaeology Service excavating the burial. (ASWYAS)

SWYOR-C4F166 (2007 T388): The
main urn from the burial group
with an accessory vessel and
the polished stone mace head.
(ASWYAS)

A second urn from the burial.
(ASWYAS)

8. Copper-alloy rapier (SWYOR-7A4C37)
Bronze Age, *c.* 1300–1140 BC
Discovered in 2011 in Hackforth, North Yorkshire.

This object is remarkable, as it is almost complete despite being over 3,000 years old. Although it is in three pieces, the breaks happened after it was deposited in the ground. The missing handle would probably have been made of an organic material that has not survived.

The rapier is a two-edged thrusting weapon, though it may not have been used in conflict. Many examples found ritually placed in wet places were too fragile for functional use, and so seem to have been made for display or ceremonial activity. Examples that were carefully repaired before they were buried suggest that they had high value too. Often, objects ritually deposited in the Bronze Age were deliberately broken or bent, but this does not seem to be the case here, which raises the question: why was this high-value and complete object buried? Could it have been an accidental loss, or was it deliberate?

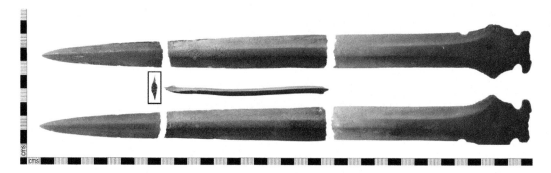

SWYOR-7A4C37: A copper-alloy rapier from Hackforth, North Yorkshire.

9. Copper-alloy axe-head hoard (YORYM-958D05, 2013 T583)
Bronze Age, *c.* 1000–800 BC
Discovered in 2013 in Cherry Burton, East Riding.

This late Bronze Age hoard comprises twenty-three objects and fragments, including sword fittings, axes and spearheads. The objects are relatively common in British late Bronze Age hoards, which typically consist of complete and fragmentary swords, spearheads and socketed axe heads. These socketed axe types are well known from northern England.

A notable inclusion in this hoard is an antennae-type sword pommel, of which only eight examples have been recorded in Britain. Several axes also display purposeful damage – crushing and burning – and the sockets of some axes were blocked with fragments of other axes. This treatment of hoard material, seen across Europe, could be related to recycling or to more ritualised decommissioning prior to burial.

Early hoards were thought to be ritual deposits, as they are often found near water, which is traditionally seen as a boundary between this world and the next. Later hoards have been interpreted as 'waste' hoards of broken or miscast objects, gathered together to be melted down and re-cast. They were perhaps buried for safekeeping and never recovered. The prevalence and character of this treatment deserves greater attention in future research.

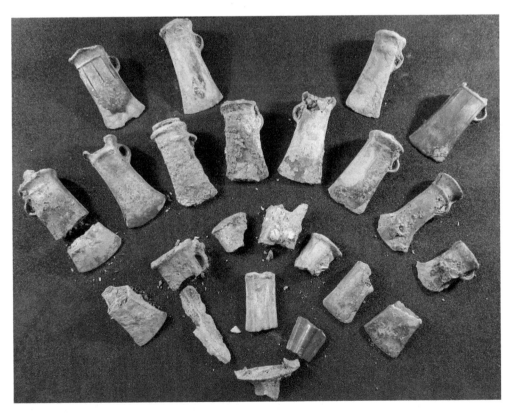

YORYM-958D05 (2013 T583): A copper-alloy Bronze Age hoard from Cherry Burton, East Riding.

Skill in metalworking continued to develop, and the technique of making iron objects was imported from the Continent, heralding the dawn of the British Iron Age. Just as the development of copper working did not make flint redundant, so the adoption of iron tools did not diminish the use of bronze. The potter's wheel, lathe and rotary quern for grinding grain were also introduced in this period.

Regional settlement patterns emerged during the Iron Age, each producing distinctive styles of pottery and metal objects. As the population increased, competition for resources led to wars between the different groups, who gradually merged until the Brigantes controlled most of Yorkshire.

Conflicts between groups may, in part, account for hillforts becoming a key feature of Iron Age Yorkshire. Over 2,000 forts are known across Britain, with Stanwick widely considered the most important in the North – perhaps even being the capital of the Brigantes tribe. It is not certain that hillforts were purely defensive, since a variety of

An Iron Age stone beehive rotary quern, used for grinding cereals. It is now on display in Wakefield Museum. (Wakefield Council)

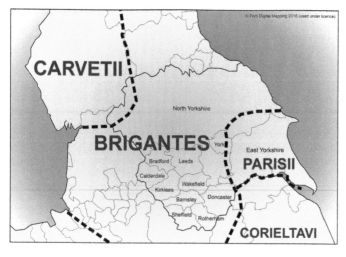

A map showing the main Iron Age territories in Yorkshire. (Ian Downes)

different activities are associated with them, including social gatherings, trade, exchange and religious activities. The importance and emphasis of certain activities at these sites may also have changed dramatically over time.

While the Brigantes controlled most of Yorkshire, Humberside was the territory of the Parisii. Commonly linked with the Parisii of Gaul, a distinct 'Arras' culture emerged in the East Riding. The name derives from the cemetery site of Arras, near Market Weighton, at which the dead were buried in square-ditched barrows, sometimes accompanied by grave goods that included wheeled vehicles. The three chariot burials at Wetwang Slack each contain a skeleton above a dismantled cart or chariot. Ferry Fryston is also a chariot burial and may be an outlier of this type of burial as it is outside the traditional Arras area.

The late Iron Age was a time of growing sophistication, as people were making increasingly elegant objects and trading with the Roman Empire. The first British coins were minted and can be seen as some of the earliest 'historical' documents, as many copy the Roman and Greek style of naming their leaders, allowing further insight into a complex period of Yorkshire's history.

A view looking up the ramparts of the Iron Age Hill Fort at Almondbury, Kirklees, with the Victorian tower at the top. (WYAAS)

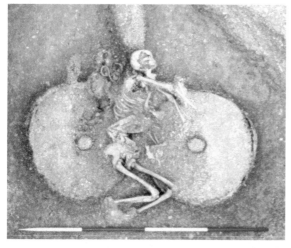

Wetwang Chariot Burial II, one of three found together during quarrying at Wetwang Slack and excavated in 1984. (Copyright Bill Marsden, courtesy of Hull and East Riding Museum, Hull Museums)

The Ferry Fryston chariot burial, Wakefield, under excavation. (Blaise Vyner)

These two gold Iron Age *staters* are inscribed with the names Dumnocoveros Tigir Seno and Volisios Dumnocoveros, who issued them (YORYM-953E38/2014 T212).

10. Copper-alloy mount (YORYM-CoBAAA)
Iron Age, *c.* 200 BC–AD 43
Discovered in 2014 in Wetwang, East Riding.

This object is unusual and appears to be unique. It is in the form of a human head, with moulded facial features and a rectangular slot at the back. The perforated eyes may have been inlaid with enamel or glass, and the slot suggests the head projected from a more or less horizontal shaft.

The function of this object is uncertain, although it has features in common with a number of objects from the same period. For example, SOMDOR-DC9D32 is a figurine head with very similar facial features, but no reverse slot.

YORYM-CoBAAA: A copper-alloy mount from Wetwang, East Riding.

A copper-alloy figurine head from the Dorchester Area, Dorset, shows similar features to the Wetwang mount (SOMDOR-DC9D32).

11. Copper-alloy strap union (SWYOR-6EE012)
Iron Age to Roman, 200 BC–AD 200
Discovered in 2011 in Wakefield.

There is often no clear distinction between objects from the late Iron Age and those from the early Roman period. In many instances, the same craftsperson was doing the work, whether under the rule of a native Briton or a Roman. While this colourful object is a good example of the sophistication of late Iron Age style, it could also be early Roman in date.

The object was probably part of a harness fitting used to connect two leather straps. It is decorated with red and yellow enamel and the shapes used are typical of the art styles of this time. This style of decoration can also be seen on an early Roman brooch from Thorpe Audlin (YORYM-D5BBD5), which is thought to be unique among Roman brooches in form and decoration.

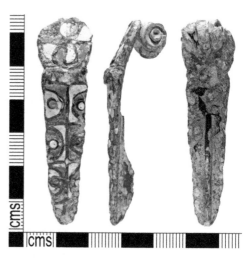

Left: SWYOR-6EE012: A copper-alloy strap union from Wakefield.

Above: A copper-alloy brooch from Thorpe Audlin, Wakefield (YORYM-D5BBD5).

12. Copper-alloy torc (SWYOR-D24682)
Iron Age to Roman, 100 BC–AD 200
Discovered in 2013 in Wadworth, Doncaster.

Another late Iron Age to early Roman object is this fragment of a beaded torc or neck ring. This example would have had a hinge and a joint known as 'mortise and tenon', comprising a hole and corresponding tongue, allowing it to fasten almost seamlessly.

When new, the bronze would have had a golden colour and been comparable to examples made from gold. It seems that torcs had particular significance to Iron Age people, beyond just bodily ornamentation and a conspicuous display of wealth. They are thought to identify people of high rank.

Beaded torcs like this one, cast in solid pieces but designed to look like separate beads, are generally only found in northern England, while gold examples are more common in the south.

SWYOR-D24682: A copper-alloy beaded torc fragment from Wadworth, Doncaster.

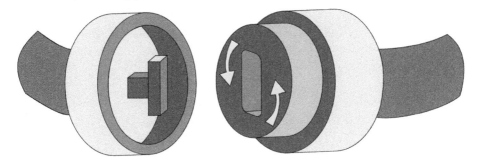

A diagram showing a mortise and tenon fastening used on a torc. The T-shaped tenon was inserted into the slot or mortise, and the component rotated to capture the tenon and fasten the torc. The Wadworth torc would have been made in several pieces, with a hinge and similar fixing to allow it to be clasped around the neck while appearing to be a solid ring. (Ian Downes)

13. Copper-alloy sword pommel (SWYOR-B546D5)
Iron Age to Roman, AD 1–100
Discovered in 2015 in Thorpe in Balne, Doncaster.

This unusual-looking fragmentary object is the pommel of a late Iron Age or early Romano-British sword. The square void in the lower end is where the iron tang of the sword would have fitted (the grip would have been immediately below this pommel), and the circular opening at the other end is a fixing for a separate knob or enamelled inset.

Similar swords with decorative bossed roundels are known, including one from Wetwang Slack. This form of pommel, with short arms extending from a central stem, is also known from Kirkburn and sites in North Yorkshire. It is interesting that many of these parallels are from northern Britain.

Above: SWYOR-B546D5: A copper-alloy sword pommel from Balne, Doncaster.

Left: Detail of the hilt from the sword buried with Wetwang Chariot Burial I. The circular bosses are similar in style to the Thorpe in Balne pommel. (Hull and East Riding Museum, Hull Museums; accession number: KINCM:2010.8.31)

14. Copper-alloy pinhead (YORYM-12C251)
Iron Age, 300–100 BC
Discovered in 2011 in Spofforth, North Yorkshire.

This copper-alloy pin is something of an enigma. The head is made up of four circular lobes with raised edges, creating deep cells that would probably have been filled with enamel or coral. A long attachment rod projects from the reverse, although it is broken.

Ring-headed pins used as dress or hair ornamentation, such as LANCUM-5ECCE3, are characteristic of the British and Irish Iron Ages and are common finds in England.

British and Irish ring-headed pins originate in the early Iron Age and are known to take a variety of forms, from plain rings to more abstract ring designs including zoomorphic (animal shaped) forms. The Spofforth example, however, is unusual, as the only currently known parallels originate in Ireland and are described by Becker and Channing (2008) as the product of a separate and independent development in Ireland.

Above: YORYM-12C251: A copper-alloy pinhead from Spofforth, North Yorkshire.

Right: A copper-alloy ring-headed pin from Leyburn, North Yorkshire, representing a more typical swan-neck pin (LANCUM-5ECCE3).

33

Chapter 2
Roman

Yorkshire was part of the Roman Empire for nearly 400 years, and it was during this period that the region began to establish itself as of central importance to Britain.

When the Romans arrived in AD 48, what is now Yorkshire was occupied by two British groups: the Brigantes, who controlled most of the north, and the Parisii in the East Riding. It is generally assumed that the Roman occupation enforced changes upon the native population, but increasingly it is being seen as a period of mixing, adaptation and development, creating a distinctive Romano-British culture. British objects generally did not show drastic shifts in design, but rather a gradual incorporation of new styles. More noticeable changes include the rise of civil engineering and the development of larger road networks, alongside the importing of pottery and coinage from the continent.

The first Roman forts in Yorkshire were established at Templeborough and Rossington Bridge in the mid-first century AD, following expeditions from territory further south that was already under Roman rule. Previously, the Brigantian leader Cartimandua had supported the Romans but, when her tribe turned against her, the Romans felt it was time to stamp their authority on the area and the forts probably date from this time. The

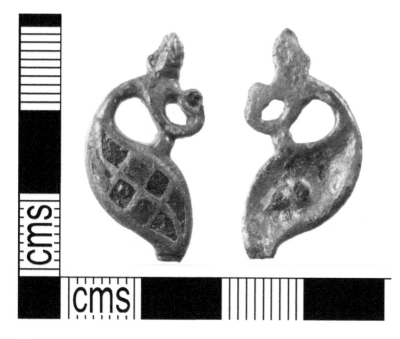

A copper-alloy dragonesque brooch from Burton Salmon, North Yorkshire, showing the continuation of Iron Age motifs on Roman artefacts (SWYOR-0E6FC5).

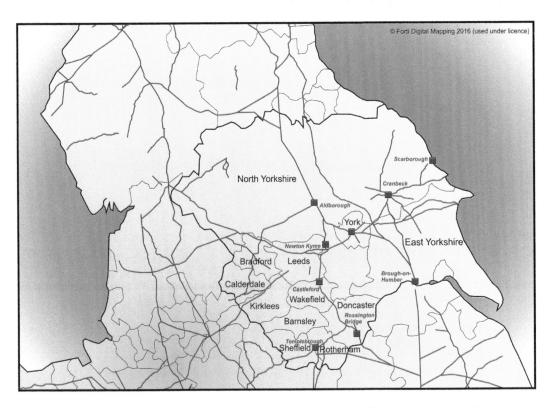

A map showing Roman roads overlaying the modern county boundaries of Yorkshire and the Roman sites mentioned in the text. (Ian Downes)

Romans finally took permanent control of the north in AD 71, building the fortress at York and making *Eboracum*, as they called the city, their northern centre. The road system was extended and improved to join the network of forts with the fortress. *Eboracum* was ideally placed to allow easy transportation of troops and supplies from the North Sea along the Ouse. It was also accessible by land, sitting on a ridge that the Romans used as their main approach to the city. This route is still largely followed by the A64 today. In fact, many major modern routes follow roads established by the Romans.

On sites unaffected by the Roman military, local manufacturing probably continued much as before, even selling products to the newcomers. Military bases were hives of industry that used a wide variety of materials, techniques and craftsmen, as well as recruiting labourers from the native population. Domestic manufacturing increased in the second century, with evidence of pottery making at various sites, including Doncaster, while the only known glassworks in Roman Britain was at Coppergate in York. In the fourth century, as imported goods declined in number, further local manufacturing emerged, such as the pottery industry at Crambeck.

In the mid-second century, administration centres were established at Aldborough and Brough on Humber, mirroring the earlier centres of power for the Brigantes and Parisii, while York remained the military headquarters of the northern Empire. Outside the forts and their civilian settlements, the roundhouse remained the most common building type; however, Roman-style stone buildings, known as villas, also appeared.

Left: A fragment of a grinding bowl (*mortaria*) dating from AD 140–160, made at Rossington Bridge, Doncaster, showing the name stamps of *SARRIUVS*, the principal potter, and *SETIBOGIVS*, the apprentice. It is held in the collection of Doncaster Museum and was photographed with their kind permission.

Below: A silver *denarius* of Septimius Severus from Aberford, Leeds (SWYOR-28BC52).

York became internationally significant in AD 208, when Septimius Severus used it as a base from which to launch his military campaigns in Scotland. His expeditions were unsuccessful and, in AD 211, he fell ill and died in York. Following Severus's death, his son Caracalla divided Britain into two provinces: the southern was *Britannia Superior*, and the northern *Britannia Inferior*, with York as its capital. In AD 306, Constantius I became the second emperor to die in York, with his son Constantine immediately claiming power. Constantine I was crowned emperor in York in the same year.

Towards the end of the Roman period, as Roman rule faltered under threat from various 'barbarian' tribes, both major settlements and rural sites declined. Signal stations – large, square timber and stone towers and courtyards surrounded by huge stone walls – were established on the east coast of Yorkshire to combat these threats. They were used as look-out posts, each with a beacon at the top of the tower, to send warnings of potential attacks.

By AD 402, no coinage was reaching Britain, suggesting that the army was not being paid, and gradually the Roman army was withdrawn, with the last forces leaving in AD 407. Though the Romans withdrew, enough of their influence remains, in architecture and infrastructure, and archaeologically, for us to gain a glimpse of life in Roman Yorkshire.

The Multangular Tower at the west corner of the Roman legionary fortress at York, as shown in a print dating from 1807 by Joseph Halfpenny. (York Museums Trust (Art Gallery) [CC By-SA 4.0] accession number: YORAG:R2351)

15. Copper-alloy coin hoard (DUR-16C89F, 2014 T645)
Roman, AD 268–307
Discovered in 2015 in Wold Newton, East Riding.

Found in a near-complete vessel, this hoard comprises denominations known as *nummi* (of which there were 1,856) and *radiates* (of which there was one). The hoard displays a mixture of emperors, mints and reverse types, and the coins are of the large, heavy type introduced by Emperor Diocletian. It is the largest hoard of this date from northern Britannia. Only one larger hoard of this period is known from Britain (Fyfield, Berkshire), which was found in 1944.

The emperors represented within the hoard have strong links to the north, and to York in particular. Many are of Constantius I, who died in York on 25 July AD 306. He was the emperor of the western empire, responsible for defeating the breakaway Britannic empire of Allectus and reuniting Britain with the rest of the empire. The latest coins are early issues of Constantine the Great, dating to AD 307 and allowing us to determine the year in which the hoard was probably buried. Many of the coins were struck at the large mint in London.

The hoard was lifted whole and 'excavated' in the British Museum. Nine different levels were removed, which gives a sense of the construction of the hoard, showing that different bags of money were mixed together; it hints at how and why the coins were concealed. This excavation also revealed insect remains that may, following proper analysis, indicate the time of year in which the hoard was buried.

DUR-16C89F (2014 T645): A copper-alloy coin hoard from Wold Newton, East Riding.

16. Copper-alloy military diploma (YORYM-67D811)
Roman, AD 118
Discovered in 2008 in Brompton, North Yorkshire and acquired by the Yorkshire Museum; YORYM:2008.171.

A detailed glimpse into the life of an individual is provided by this military diploma. Diplomas granted privileges to auxiliary soldiers who had completed their military service, which was usually of twenty-five years. This diploma was issued to an infantry solider of *Cohors V Raetorum,* but his name is lost, and it states that the individual and his descendants are granted citizenship and right of legal marriage. The emperor Hadrian is named, along with the soldier's commanding officer Sextus Cornelius Dexter of Saldae in Mauretania (modern Morocco). This diploma is copied from a bronze tablet at the Temple of the Divine Augustus, in the Forum in Rome. Enough remains of the date and sequence of military units to attribute this object to 17 July AD 118.

This diploma represents an important addition to the few known from Britain. Only two are recorded with the PAS, while another thirteen are held by the British Museum (including one from Sheffield and one from York). The detail preserved in this object is exceptional and the provision of such a precise date for a non-coin object is incredibly rare.

YORYM-67D811: A fragmentary copper-alloy military diploma from 'Near Scarborough', North Yorkshire. (York Museums Trust (Yorkshire Museum) [CC By-SA 4.0] accession number: YORYM:2008.171)

A view across the Forum in Rome, where the tablet bearing the inscription that was copied on to the diploma would have been displayed.

17. Copper-alloy knife handle (SWYOR-374234)
Roman, AD 43–200
Discovered in 2011 in Askham Bryan, York.

This handle from a fixed-blade knife is a very good example of the Roman appreciation of erotic and graphic decoration. Though badly corroded, it depicts a couple engaged in making love, the woman crouched on top of a reclining male. It is one of only five erotic knife handles recorded with the PAS and, interestingly, it is only the second example depicting two people: the other was sold by Christies in 1998. Most other such knives depict scenes involving three people, and some involve a decapitated head as well.

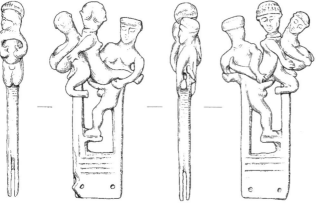

Above: SWYOR-374234: A copper-alloy knife handle from Askham Bryan, York.

Left: A copper-alloy erotic knife handle from Syston, Lincolnshire, showing three figures, two male and one female, engaged in sexual intercourse. The smaller male figure also holds a decapitated head (LIN-536F87).

18. Copper-alloy button and loop fastener (WMID-998297)
Roman, AD 50–150
Discovered in 2013 in Sherburn, North Yorkshire.

Button and loop fasteners are perhaps best interpreted as multi-purpose fasteners for use with harness equipment, as well as clothing. They are thought to be military objects, though the PAS examples tend to be found on rural sites not specifically related to military activity.

The number of recorded examples of button and loop fasteners has increased significantly through the PAS, and previously unrecorded variants such as this 'double-headed' type have been identified. Few double-headed examples have been published, and only twenty-two have been recorded with the PAS. Almost all of these are from northern counties, and one was found in the Scottish Traprain Law Hoard, which is thought to be a haul looted from Yorkshire by Pictish raiders. The relatively restricted distribution of these objects may reflect an aspect of regional identity specific to the north.

WMID-998297: A copper-alloy double-headed button and loop fastener from Sherburn, North Yorkshire.

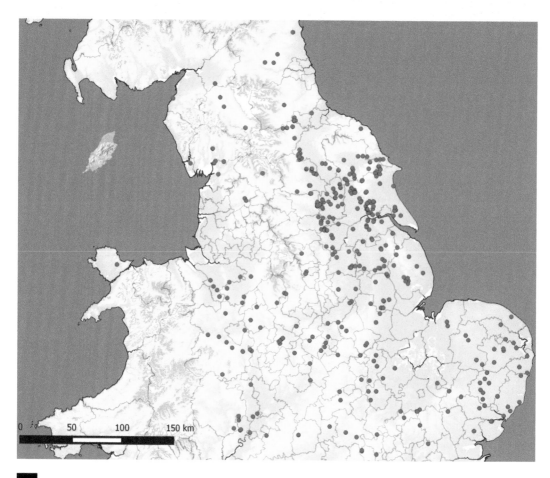

Above: A map showing the distribution of double-headed button and loop fasteners (red dots) compared to the findspots of all button and loop fasteners recorded by the PAS (blue dots).

Left: A copper-alloy double-headed button and loop fastener from South Cave, East Riding (YORYM-AC7061).

19. Copper-alloy headstud brooch set (YORYM-5589D6)
Roman, AD 75–200
Discovered in 2007 in Sancton, East Riding.

Headstud brooches are one of the most common, best-known and longest-lived brooch types from Roman Britain. Characterised by their solid, arched bow with a decorative knop, the headstud brooch was a native British type, probably manufactured by groups of travelling craftsmen, and is most frequently found in the north of England. Excavations at Castleford revealed a major Roman metalworking industry that produced high-status enamelled flasks and spoons, and the discovery of unfinished headstud brooches, such as SWYOR-92A6C9, suggests that brooches were also made there. Unpublished examples of brooches bearing inscriptions reading *Fibula ex regione Lagitiense* ('brooch from the region of Castleford') further support this theory.

New variations within the headstud type are also becoming apparent through PAS data. Brooches with two knops have recently been found in Yorkshire and Lincolnshire, and were thought to be a northern phenomenon until the recent recording of one from the Isle of Wight changed our thinking.

YORYM-5589D6: A copper-alloy headstud brooch set from Sancton, East Riding.

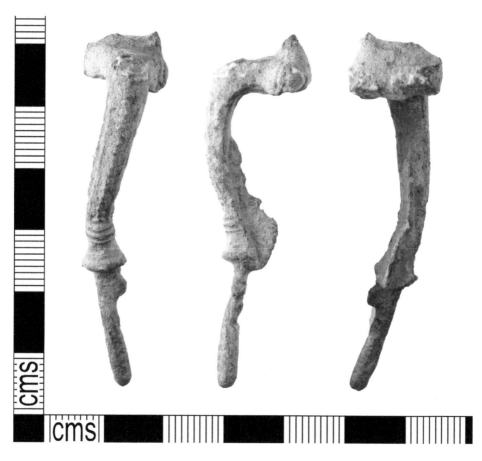

A copper-alloy unfinished headstud brooch from Featherstone, Wakefield, which was probably made at Castleford. The casting sprue and seams have not been trimmed (SWYOR-92A6C9).

A copper-alloy double headstud brooch from Brantingham, East Riding (YORYM-EDE045).

20. Glass bangle fragment (YORYM-B985BA)
Roman, AD 43–200
Discovered in 2015 in Kilham, East Riding.

Bracelets and bangles of a variety of materials, including metal, jet and shale, are a particularly common find on Romano-British sites. Glass examples such as this were popular in the early first to mid-second century. To create them, molten glass would be rolled out on a cool surface such as marble; the main bracelet would have to maintain a temperature that would allow the second piece, the darker strip, to be added without causing the glass to shatter. Despite this, such bracelets were easy and fast to manufacture. Their use remains unclear and, while it is possible that they were worn as arm or leg ornaments, they may also have had a more specialised use that is not currently understood.

YORYM-B985BA: A glass bangle fragment from Kilham, East Yorkshire.

21. Copper-alloy and glass *millefiore* disc brooch (SWYOR-0F6696)
Roman, AD 150–300
Found in 2014 in Wighill, North Yorkshire.

Another example of the Romans' skill with glassworking is this beautiful disc, probably part of a brooch, but possibly from a mount. The chequerboard pattern is formed from tiny rods of glass bound into bundles, a technique called *millefiore* (an Italian word meaning 'a thousand flowers'). The technique was developed by the Romans, and was only used on high-status objects as it is so labour intensive and therefore expensive.

SWYOR-0F6696: A copper-alloy and glass *millefiore* disc brooch from Wighill, North Yorkshire.

22. Copper-alloy and silver hoard (YORYM-5EFF04, 2005 T268)
Roman, AD 43–300
Discovered in 2005 near Tadcaster, North Yorkshire, and acquired by the Yorkshire Museum; YORYM:2007.6299.

While numerous coin hoards are known throughout the Roman Empire, there are more from Britain than from any other province in the Empire. This example is particularly interesting, as it contains a copper-alloy arm-purse and lamp, as well as the four silver coins.

Arm-purses appear to have been male and military accessories, with examples found in auxiliary and legionary contexts in Britain and on the Continent.

The coins represent the emperors Domitian (AD 81–96), Trajan (AD 98–117), Marcus Aurelius (AD 161–80), and Commodus (AD 180–92). They could have been a random selection from the Antonine period; however, having one of each emperor could also suggest the burial was a deliberate, possibly ritual, act.

The lamp depicts a female head, possibly a *Maenad* (an immortal female follower of Dionysus, the god of ritual madness and ecstasy), so the lamp being in the hoard may further support the idea that the hoard is a ritual offering.

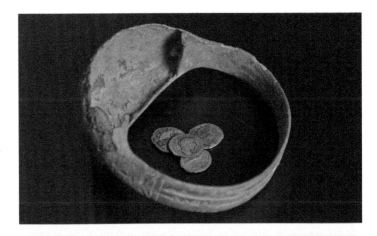

YORYM-5EFF04 (2005 T268): A silver coin hoard with a copper-alloy arm-purse from the Tadcaster Area, York. (York Museums Trust (Yorkshire Museum) [CC By-SA 4.0] accession number: YORYM:2007.6299)

The copper-alloy lamp found with the arm-purse and coins from the Tadcaster Area, York (YORYM-5EFF04). (York Museums Trust (Yorkshire Museum) [CC By-SA 4.0] accession number: YORYM:2007.6299)

23. Copper-alloy figurine of Cautopates (SWYOR-9FCBB3)
Roman, AD 43–307
Discovered in 2007 at Newton Kyme cum Toulston, North Yorkshire.

This figurine is linked to the eastern cult of Mithras, a religion that was very popular among Roman soldiers and merchants, especially in the second and third centuries, until Constantine legalised Christianity.

It depicts Cautopates, one of the two attendants of Mithras; Cautopates holds a downward-pointing torch symbolising darkness, death and night, while Cautes, his opposite, is an emblem of light, day and life, and holds his torch upwards.

The secretive Mithraic cult was based on a creation myth. Mithras was sent to earth to slay a divine bull in a cave; all life sprang from its shed blood. Worshippers gathered in semi-underground temples symbolising the cave, decorated with scenes of the sacrifice, for feasting and ritual initiation ceremonies. Temples had to be near water for purification purposes, and women were banned from the cult.

Several Mithraic temples are known on Hadrian's Wall, with some at other forts and at London and York. However, very few metallic votive items are known, and it has not been possible to find a direct parallel for this figurine.

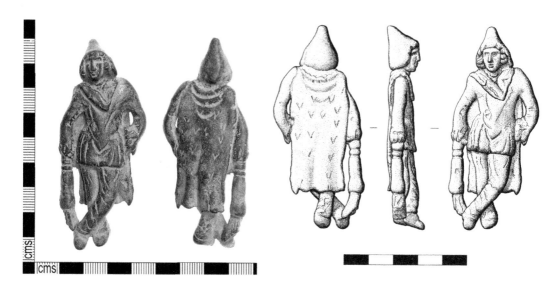

Left: SWYOR-9FCBB3: A copper-alloy figurine of Cautopates from Newton Kyme Cum Toulston, North Yorkshire.

Right: An illustration of the Cautopates figurine SWYOR-9FCBB3.

24. Copper-alloy manicure set (SWYOR-C74924)
Roman, AD 43–200
Discovered in 2013 in Fangfoss, East Riding.

Another object with religious connections is this manicure kit in the form of a cockerel. The figurine is a chatelaine (a decorative bar or hook), from which various personal grooming tools would have hung. Personal grooming and hygiene was important to the Romans, as can be seen from bathhouses and the evidence of make-up and perfumes.

The cockerel represents Mercury, one of the gods most commonly depicted on objects recorded with the PAS. Mercury was the messenger god, linked to cockerels because they heralded the new day. This manicure set demonstrates how religion was fully integrated into every aspect of Roman life.

The tools that formed the set probably included a nail cleaner, tweezers and perhaps a cosmetic pestle and mortar.

Above: SWYOR-C74924: A copper-alloy manicure set, in the form of a cockerel, from Fangfoss, East Riding.

Right: An illustration of a complete manicure set found at Castleford, Wakefield. It includes two nail cleaners, a file, tweezers, an ear-scoop or cosmetic spoon and a notched blade. (WYAAS)

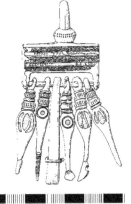

49

25. Copper-alloy statue fragment (YORYM-F46085)
Roman, AD 43–410
Discovered in 2013 in Terrington, North Yorkshire.

This fragment is one of twelve from an approximately life-sized statue of a human figure, although it is not clear whether it depicts an emperor, a god, or an idealised figure bearing realistic features.

Detailed assessment revealed that the pieces must have suffered severe damage at some point in the past for unknown reasons, with the separately made iris and pupil appearing to have been intentionally and violently detached from their corresponding cavities.

A similarly treated statue, though of a horse, was found in North Carlton, Lincolnshire. The record (LIN-31B698) suggests that the statue may have been dismantled and removed for re-melting. The same is likely for the Yorkshire example. The findspots, close to urban and military sites, suggest their possible displacement from public spaces in towns or garrisons.

YORYM-F46085: A copper-alloy statue fragment from Terrington, North Yorkshire. This eye fragment was found first, with a number of other fragments from the same statue subsequently discovered.

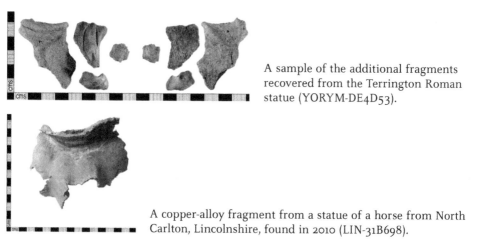

A sample of the additional fragments recovered from the Terrington Roman statue (YORYM-DE4D53).

A copper-alloy fragment from a statue of a horse from North Carlton, Lincolnshire, found in 2010 (LIN-31B698).

26. Copper-alloy dodecahedron (YORYM-41CD72)
Roman, AD 43–410.
Discovered in 2008 in Fridaythorpe, East Riding.

One of the more unusual finds from Roman Britain is this dodecahedron: a hollow, twelve-sided object. Dodecahedrons appear to be restricted to the northern part of the Empire, stretching from Britain to Hungary, and have been found in contexts that range from the first to fourth centuries AD. The findspots are also diverse, including military camps, graves, and rivers. Few are known from Britain and only four others are recorded with the PAS.

The function of dodecahedrons remains uncertain – suggestions include surveying instruments, rangefinders, candleholders, astronomical measuring devices or polygonal dice. A further suggestion is that they are sceptre heads, but 'the argument is not conclusive and further evidence is required for these enigmatic items to be fully understood' (Allason-Jones and Miket, 1984).

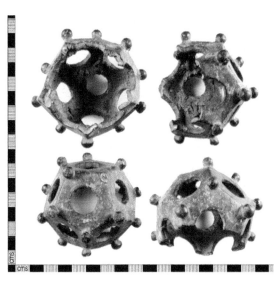

YORYM-41CD72: A copper-alloy
dodecahedron from Fridaythorpe, East
Riding.

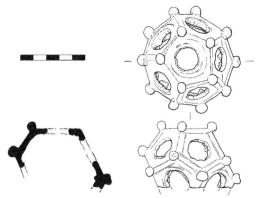

An illustration of the Fridaythorpe
dodecahedron.

Chapter 3
Early Medieval

The time after the Roman withdrawal and before the Norman invasion is known archaeologically as the Early Medieval period, and can be further subdivided into the Anglian (AD 410–866) and Anglo-Scandinavian or Viking (AD 866–1066) periods. It includes a short length of post-Roman indigenous rule and ends with the unification of England into a single kingdom. The objects recorded from this period are many and varied, displaying the different decorative styles of distinct cultures.

The immediate post-Roman era is unclear archaeologically, as native Britons under Roman rule are virtually indistinguishable from those ruling themselves. How long, and in what form, Roman structures of administration persisted after the army left is unclear. An ever-shifting, complex pattern of small, warring kingdoms emerged.

Following the Roman withdrawal, Yorkshire was attacked by Picts, Scots and Anglo-Saxon raiders. The Germanic invaders consisted of two main groups: the Angles (or Anglians) from modern north Germany, and the Saxons from the modern German-Dutch border. The Angles settled in eastern Britain, including Deira (modern East Yorkshire) and East Anglia, while the Saxons adopted territory further south. Deira was disputed territory claimed by both Angles and Saxons. It eventually joined with Bernicia, to the north, to form a single kingdom of Northumbria, which stretched from the Humber to south-east Scotland. Following battles in Hatfield and Winwaed (believed to be in Yorkshire) in the seventh century, the unified kingdom expanded, incorporating Elmet and uniting Yorkshire and the wider north.

During this period, aristocratic status was defined by the ability to muster wealth and give extravagant gifts to other leaders. Some of the objects in this chapter reflect this gift-giving tradition. The Anglo-Saxon fashion for objects of gold and garnet is clearly demonstrated in the famous Staffordshire Hoard.

By the mid-ninth century, England had unified into four independent kingdoms: East Anglia, Wessex, Mercia and Northumbria. From the late eighth century, it suffered sporadic attacks by Scandinavian raiders known as Vikings. In AD 865, the Great Danish Army, led by Ivar the Boneless, landed in East Anglia, seeking new territories. This was not a band of opportunists, but a large and organised army. Heading north, they seized York, which was a prosperous trading settlement, and made it their capital, Jorvik. The Vikings eventually took control of the Anglo-Saxon kingdoms and, by AD 874, only Wessex, ruled by Alfred the Great, remained under Anglo-Saxon control. Ultimately, England was divided into the Anglo-Saxon south-west and the Viking north-east, known as the Danelaw.

While popular perception suggests that the Vikings were attacking and conquering raiders, there is a range of evidence suggesting that they were also farmers, traders and craftspeople. Increasingly we are learning that Vikings were very adaptable, raiding and trading interchangeably.

The Anglo-Saxon leader Athelstan succeeded to the kingdom of Northumbria in AD 927, becoming the first king of England with authority over all of Britain. This is celebrated on coins, which use the title: *'Rex TOtius BRItanniaE'* ('King of all Britons').

Almost ninety years later, Cnut the Great, king of Denmark, Sweden and Norway, conquered England, placing Yorkshire under Viking rule once again, along with the rest

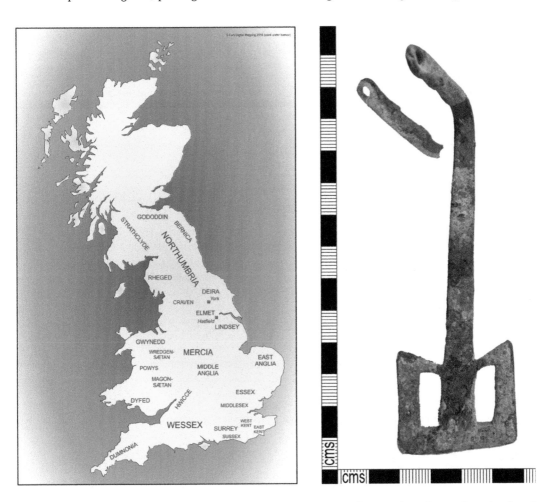

Left: A map showing some of the post-Roman, Anglian and Saxon kingdoms of England and Wales. (Ian Downes)

Right: Several object types are distinctively Anglian, including this girdle hanger from Kilham, East Riding. Girdle hangers date from the sixth century and are associated with Anglian women. They appear to be imitation keys or latch-lifters, which were worn suspended from a belt. They may have emphasised the woman's status as mistress of the household (FAKL-508584).

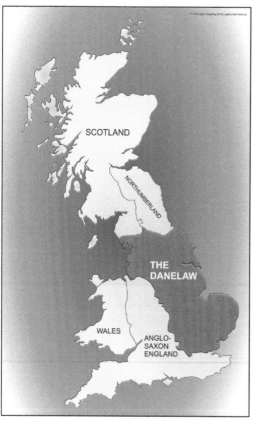

Above: Some of the stunning artefacts from the Staffordshire Hoard. Many of the objects in the hoard would have been given as gifts to reinforce the social status of the giver and recipient. (WMID-oB5416/2009T394; for more information see http://finds.org.uk/staffshoardsymposium)

Left: A map showing the Danelaw and the Anglo-Saxon part of England. (Ian Downes)

of England this time. Cnut's empire, bridging the North Sea, made him one of the most powerful men in Europe.

In AD 1066, following the death of Edward the Confessor, Harold Godwinson became king of England. He defeated a Scandinavian army seeking to reclaim Cnut's kingdom at the Battle of Stamford Bridge in September of the same year, allowing William of Normandy to take advantage of the distraction and invade the south coast. Weakened by his exploits in the north, Harold was defeated just nineteen days after the Battle of Stamford Bridge by William at the Battle of Hastings. This event was the turning point that marks the end of the Early Medieval period.

A penny describing Athelstan as 'King of all Britons' with the legend *EÐELSTAN REX TO BRIE*. This coin was recovered from the Vale of York Hoard. (York Museums Trust (Yorkshire Museum) [CC By-SA 4.0] accession number YORYM:2009.55.639)

The death of Harold at the Battle of Hastings, as depicted on the Bayeux Tapestry. (Myrabella (Own work) [Public domain or CC0], https://commons.wikimedia.org/wiki/File:Bayeux_Tapestry_scene57_Harold_death.jpg)

27. Copper-alloy, gold and iron burial assemblage (BM-7C4457, 2011 T300)
Early Medieval, AD 600–700
Discovered in 2011 in Middleham, North Yorkshire, and acquired by the Yorkshire
Museum; YORYM:2015.567.

This group is a grave assemblage from a single Anglian burial of the seventh century AD.
The assemblage comprises a sword, pommel, spearhead, knife, hanging-bowl fragments –
including escutcheons and a ring – and a gold shilling coin. Such objects form a standard
assemblage from a single burial.

While the majority of the objects can only be broadly dated to the sixth or seventh
centuries, the coin can be dated to around AD 625–640. The inclusion of hanging bowls
in otherwise weapon-based burials is not uncommon, and the fashion for including them
appears to last throughout the seventh century (Geake, 1999).

The objects contained within the hoard are elaborate, reflecting a high-status individual
displaying his wealth even after death. The find is significant, as it is the most elaborately
furnished Anglian burial in northern England and contains the only known English gold
shilling from a burial context.

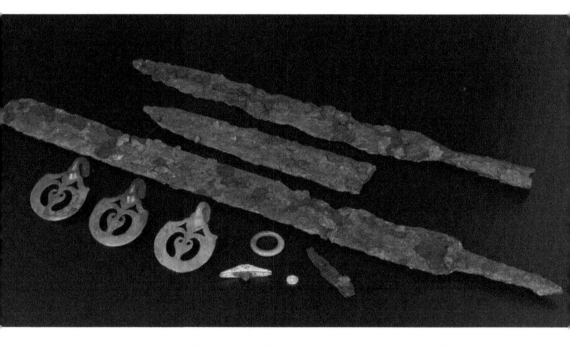

BM-7C4457 (2011 T300): Items from the Anglian burial assemblage from Middleham, North
Yorkshire. (York Museums Trust (Yorkshire Museum) [CC By-SA 4.0] accession number
YORYM:2015.567)

28. Copper-alloy *Pressblech* die (DUR-3C5813)
Early Medieval, AD 570–700
Discovered in 2011 in Thwing, East Riding.

Elaborate decoration is common in the Early Medieval period, and this *Pressblech* die for making impressed foil mounts demonstrates one technique employed. The decoration features intertwined lines, known as interlace, that represent the bodies of animals – in this case, predatory birds with elongated, curved beaks. This type of design was widely used in the seventh century.

Pressblech is the name for the metal foils that are used to decorate objects such as helmets, drinking horns and jewellery. The foils are produced by beating a thin sheet of metal over a die bearing the desired pattern. The die itself is the more difficult item to produce, as the designs are painstakingly hand carved.

Of particular interest regarding this die was the discovery of a lead trial piece from Selby (YORYM-D6E0A2). Comparisons of the two pieces show that this impression was made by the die found over 40 miles away.

Above left: DUR-3C5813: A copper-alloy *Pressblech* die from Thwing, East Riding.

Above right: A lead-alloy trial piece from North Duffield, North Yorkshire, which is impressed with the design from the die DUR-3C5813. It was probably used to cushion the foil of precious metal while it was hammered onto the die (YORYM-D6E0A2).

Right: The Benty Grange helmet was discovered in 1848 in an Anglo-Saxon barrow in Monyash, Derbyshire. It is now in the collection of Museums Sheffield. The gaps between the iron frame would have been filled with horn plates, which would have been covered with *pressblech* foils for decoration. (Museums Sheffield)

29. Gold and garnet pendant (YORYM214)
Early Medieval, AD 620–660
Discovered in 1965 in Holderness, East Riding and acquired by the Ashmolean Museum.

A stunning example of jewellery is this Anglo-Saxon cross pendant, made from gold *cloisonné* work and inlaid with garnets. *Cloisonné* is a decorative technique in which small compartments are created from strips or wires of metal, with enamel, glass or garnet set in the resulting cells.

Three similar examples of gold crosses, known as the St Cuthbert, Wilton and Ixworth crosses, share numerous features with the Holderness Cross. Each bear *cloisonné* garnet inlays within cells of varied shapes, and have flaring arms. This allows the Holderness Cross to be dated to the mid-seventh century, making it an early example of such a cross.

YORYM214: A gold and garnet pendant from Holderness, East Riding.

30. Gold shilling coin (SWYOR-62B752)
Early Medieval, AD 640–660
Discovered in 2012 in 'Harrogate', North Yorkshire.

Gold coins are always exciting finds, as few are discovered, but this one is particularly special as it is the first example known of a new type. The coin is a shilling (also known as a *thrymsa*) minted in York. The previously discovered examples fall into three categories, but this one bears a different design and so was classified as a new type. Remarkably, the same findspot also produced another coin of the same type (SWYOR-7D3B1D), suggesting the two may be part of a scattered hoard.

Only nineteen examples of the York group of gold shillings are known. These were struck in the early seventh century, and were the first coinage ever made in York. Until recently, their attribution to a mint in York was uncertain, but recent finds, which show a clear Yorkshire focus, have made this very likely.

The obverse (front) image of a standing figure holding two crosses is thought to reflect religious beliefs of the time, which held that the symbol of the cross could ward off evil. The coin is also an indicator of high status, being used not for simple monetary exchange, but rather as a status symbol and for gift-giving among the elite.

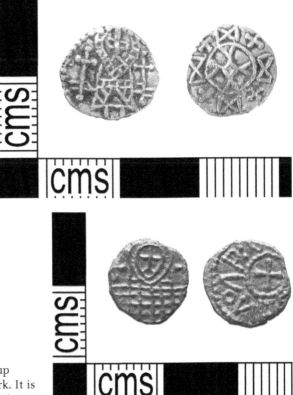

SWYOR-62B752: A gold seventh-century shilling or *thrymsa* coin from 'Harrogate', North Yorkshire, of a previously unknown type – it is now classified as York Group Type D.

One of the nineteen known York Group shillings; this one is from Fulford, York. It is of York Group Type C (YORYM-504283).

31. Gold and garnet jewellery hoard (SWYOR-F86A02, 2008 T553 and SWYOR-3B5652, 2009 T221)

Early Medieval, AD 600–1100

Discovered in 2008 and 2009 in 'West Yorkshire' and acquired by Leeds Museums and Galleries.

This hoard contains an interesting mix of spectacular objects and incomplete items of different dates. It comprises four gold finger rings, a partial gold ingot, and a broken piece of *cloisonné* jewellery. The *cloisonné* fragment is datable to the early seventh century, while the two largest rings are from the tenth century and of the highest quality known from Anglo-Saxon England. These pieces are exceptional and certainly belonged to someone of high status. Their inclusion in a hoard with lower-quality objects is puzzling. One possibility is that the hoard belonged to a thief who repeatedly added to and possibly removed from it over time. This is supported through the excavation of the findspot, which revealed that the hole in which the hoard was buried had been opened and reburied several times.

SWYOR-F86A02 (2008 T553) and SWYOR-3B5652 (2009 T221); the West Yorkshire Hoard, and a spindle whorl found in the same location. The hoard is now on display at Leeds City Museum. (Leeds Museums and Galleries)

Another very high quality tenth-century gold finger ring is this example from 'Near York', acquired by the Yorkshire Museum. It is comparable with the West Yorkshire Hoard examples, though it is set with a sapphire rather than a garnet (YORYM-715F42/2009T223). (York Museums Trust (Yorkshire Museum) [CC By-SA 4.0] accession number YORYM:2011.262)

32. Iron weaving batten (SWYOR-EB10D8)
Early Medieval, AD 800–900
Discovered in 2011 in Kettlewell, North Yorkshire.

At first glance, this object looks like a sword, but is in fact a tool used in the production of textiles. The batten was used to pack strands of yarn tightly together and was used primarily by women. The skills employed in this process are likely to have been passed down from generation to generation. The presence of battens in graves suggests that they were prized possessions, possibly of fairly high status.

The form of this batten is characteristic of examples from northern England, which have a socketed attachment rather than a tang, as in southern examples. This object is one of the first pieces of evidence for the wool industry of Yorkshire, which became so important in the Medieval period.

Above: SWYOR-EB10D8: An iron weaving batten from Kettlewell, North Yorkshire, which would have been straight when in use.

Right: Diagram of how the weaving batten would have been used with a warp weighted loom to beat the threads upwards, packing them tightly together.

33. Lead and copper-alloy weight (SWYOR-D00CF2)
Early Medieval, AD 837–900
Discovered in 2010 in Walton.

Weights are one of the objects most commonly recorded with the PAS (with nearly 1,400 from Yorkshire alone), but are often very difficult to date and interpret. The different systems of weight measurements are difficult to understand when they are from periods in which they were not documented. Also, some weights do not fit into any of the recognised systems, but were instead made for individual specific uses.

This weight is one of the few examples that can be dated with certainty, as it has an early medieval coin from the kingdom of Northumbria embedded in it. The name of the moneyer is visible on the coin: Edelhelm, who is known to have issued coins for King Osberht (AD 848–867) and Archbishop Wigmund (AD 837–854).

Objects such as this were used to weigh out metals used in trading by incoming Vikings in the ninth century, who valued precious metals by their bullion value, weighing them on balances.

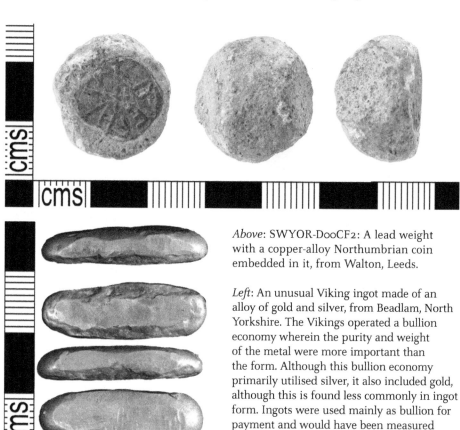

Above: SWYOR-D00CF2: A lead weight with a copper-alloy Northumbrian coin embedded in it, from Walton, Leeds.

Left: An unusual Viking ingot made of an alloy of gold and silver, from Beadlam, North Yorkshire. The Vikings operated a bullion economy wherein the purity and weight of the metal were more important than the form. Although this bullion economy primarily utilised silver, it also included gold, although this is found less commonly in ingot form. Ingots were used mainly as bullion for payment and would have been measured using weights such as SWYOR-D00CF2. (YORYM-7706AD/ 2014 T783).

34. Silver and gold hoard (SWYOR-AECB53, 2007 T2)
Early Medieval, AD 927
Discovered in 2007 in the Vale of York and acquired jointly by the British Museum, the Yorkshire Museum and Harrogate Museum.

The most significant Viking hoard discovered in 150 years, the Vale of York Hoard is nationally important. It comprises 617 coins and sixty-seven pieces of silver jewellery and ingots, buried under and within the bowl. There was also a gold arm-ring and many fragments of lead, which probably formed a lid or box.

The coins are a mixture of Viking and Anglo-Saxon issues, as well as some Islamic pieces, and are notable because so many are exceedingly rare types. The most remarkable coin names a mint that was previously unknown: Rorivacaster, although the exact location of this place is still debated.

The bowl is an ecclesiastical vessel from Frankia (modern France) and, excitingly, matching examples are known from the Halton Moor Hoard (discovered 150 years ago in Lancashire) and from the recently discovered Dumfries Hoard. The bowls are so similar that they were probably made by the same craftsperson, and may have been part of the same set, which all came to Britain together. Whether they came through trade, or were paid as tribute to the Vikings, or even were taken as loot, will never be known.

Silver hoards are characteristic of the Viking Age, and several have been discovered in Yorkshire, including the Bedale Hoard (YORYM-CEE620). The number of hoards buried during this period is a direct result of the political instability brought about in AD 869, when the Vikings conquered Northumbria and took York as their capital. The area remained under Viking control until it was conquered by Athelstan in AD 927. Athelstan destroyed York's fortifications, distributed the wealth of the city among his followers and demanded tributes in silver from the other northern leaders.

A unique silver penny naming the previously unrecorded mint of Rorivacastr. This coin was recovered from the Vale of York Hoard. (York Museums Trust (Yorkshire Museum) [CC By-SA 4.0] accession number YORYM:2009.55.671)

SWYOR-AECB53 (2007 T2): The Vale of York Hoard of 617 coins, held within the silver-gilt vessel, with a gold armband and sixty-seven silver objects, some of which were found beneath the vessel. The whole group was probably wrapped in a sheet of lead before it was buried. The Hoard was acquired jointly by the British Museum, the Yorkshire Museum and Harrogate Museum. (York Museums Trust (Yorkshire Museum) [CC By-SA 4.0] accession number YORYM:2009.55)

The Bedale Hoard from North Yorkshire comprises mostly silver ingots, as well as neck and arm rings, a brooch, and parts of an Anglo-Saxon sword decorated in Trewhiddle style. The large silver collar is unique in its design, and sheer flashiness, weighing just over 546 grams (YORYM-CEE620/2012 T373).

Chapter 4
Medieval

The Norman Conquest of AD 1066 marks the start of the Medieval period, and has been described as 'the only successful Christian conquest of England, [bringing] with it a new royal dynasty, a new aristocracy, a new Church, a new art and architecture and in official circles at least, a new language' (Rowley, 1997). Following the Battle of Hastings, northern England resisted William the Conqueror's control. He arrived in York in AD 1068 and began the construction of two castles, Clifford's Tower and Baile Hill, to control river access to the city. This afforded William some power over the area, but the people rebelled, burning the castles and massacring the garrisons. William eventually subdued the north with a series of devastating assaults, in which widespread looting, burning and slaughtering led to famine – this event became known as the 'Harrying of the North'.

William originally intended to create a balanced hierarchy of Anglo-Saxons and Normans but, due to the revolts, he replaced all English men in positions of authority with Normans. These newcomers brought new fashions with them, which is particularly evident in the architecture of Norman-style castles such as Richmond, Barlborough, and Middleham. Innovative new forms were also developed, as seen at Conisbrough Castle, for example.

Clifford's Tower now stands on the site of one of the motte-and-bailey castles built by William the Conqueror.

Left: The iconic York Minster. The first recorded church on the site was a wooden structure built in the seventh century. Today, it is one of the most recognisable landmarks in the city of York.

Right: Conisbrough Castle, Doncaster, is one of the finest examples of a late twelfth-century keep, using a design that is unique in England. The cylindrical tower with massive projecting buttresses is a pinnacle of architectural design, and is related to French styles in castle building. Conisbrough Castle is also notable for being an inspiration for Sir Walter Scott's 1819 novel *Ivanhoe*. (Philip Holmes)

The Church and religion were vitally important to medieval people, whose piety was a central aspect of their lives. A Norman replacement for the Viking minster at York was commissioned by Thomas of Bayeux, the new archbishop of York. Numerous monastic houses were also established, including St Mary's Abbey, York, which soon became one of the greatest and richest Benedictine abbeys in the north. Pilgrimage became a standard practice, and related objects such as pilgrim souvenirs are frequently found, providing a glimpse into personal devotion.

Further reflecting the importance of religion, land that had been reduced to waste by the Harrying was granted to religious houses, who founded granges (monastic farms) to oversee the repopulation of devastated areas. Rievaulx and Roche Abbeys are examples of monasteries founded in Yorkshire that still dominate the landscape today.

Repopulation was encouraged as it provided a source of funding for Norman authorities through the development of new planned settlements such as Tickhill and Scarborough, which could be taxed. Landowners profited further from these towns through market trading, which is visible in objects recorded with the PAS. Alongside coins, trade weights for measuring goods and tumbrels used to check the quality of coins are often found. Jettons (reckoning tokens used by merchants and businessmen for accounting) are another common find.

The Medieval period saw the emergence of a number of industries administered by abbeys. A thriving wool and cloth trade was centred in urban areas such as York, Ripon and Beverley, though, over time, many smaller towns became involved as the industry continued to grow. Metalworking was also embraced by monasteries. Byland Abbey, for

A lead-alloy pilgrim's ampulla from Brierley, Barnsley. It has a scallop-shell design related to pilgrimage to the shrine of St James of Santiago de Compostela in Spain, which is frequently seen on pilgrim souvenirs (SWYOR-616F31).

A copper-alloy tumbrel from Fulford, York. This portable folding balance would have been used to weigh coins to check that they contained the right amount of silver (FAKL-53A266).

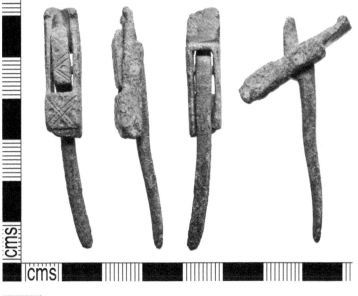

A copper-alloy fourteenth-century jetton from the Wakefield Area. This is an English type depicting the king (SWYOR-802D66).

example, was granted a licence to mine iron. The Emley bellpits (shafts dug to reach the ore and their spoilheaps) resulted from this activity, and are now a Scheduled Ancient Monument. Many of these industries and crafts that flourished in Yorkshire were organised into guilds, which supported their members as well as controlling quality and trade. By AD 1415, there were ninety-six craft guilds in York alone.

The spring of AD 1349 saw the arrival of the Black Death in Yorkshire, a county already weakened by war with Scotland. The plague's 40 per cent mortality rate caused a dramatic population decrease; this is reflected in guild records, which saw the induction of new members at a remarkable rate to replace those who had died. The plummeting population also impacted upon rural life and contributed to the abandonment of about 3,000 villages across the country. Wharram Percy on the Yorkshire Wolds is one such site, which was reduced from a thriving village of two manors to just a single farm in AD 1500.

The War of the Roses (AD 1455–1487) was Yorkshire's most significant medieval conflict, in which the two great houses of York and Lancaster fought for the throne. Much of the fighting took place in Yorkshire, including some of the most decisive engagements – for example, The Battle of Wakefield; and the bloodiest battle in English history, the Battle of Towton.

Rule eventually passed to Edward IV, and then his son Edward V, when he was only twelve. Edward's uncle Richard was named as Protector of England, but he claimed the throne for himself, imprisoning Edward V and his younger brother. The fate of these 'Princes in the Tower' remains unknown. Richard III, as he became, had firm ties to Yorkshire, spending much of his childhood at Middleham Castle and settling at Sheriff Hutton Castle. He remains a much-loved son of the city of York.

The last battle in the War of the Roses was the Battle of Bosworth in AD 1485, which saw Richard's defeat, and marks the end of the Medieval period.

Left: The ruins of Sandal Castle, Wakefield. Richard of York was safely ensconced in Sandal Castle but, on 30 December AD 1460, he was goaded by the Lancastrians into coming out to fight at the Battle of Wakefield. He was outmanoeuvred and killed.

Right: An aerial photograph of some of the Emley Bellpits, Kirklees, now a Scheduled Ancient Monument. Each mound is a spoil heap from a shaft dug to mine iron. (WYAAS)

The Merchant Adventurers' Hall in York. The Merchant Adventurers were entrepreneurs who traded goods overseas, as well as controlling trade in the city of York – for example, by checking the accuracy of weights. This building was the headquarters of their guild and was one of the most important buildings in the medieval city. Its three main rooms served the three functions of a medieval guild: business and social activities in the Great Hall, charitable work in the undercroft and religious observance in the chapel.

A view over Bloody Meadow at Towton Battlefield, North Yorkshire. In AD 1461, the bloodiest battle in English history was fought here. The Yorkists were victorious, enabling Richard of York's son Edward to displace Henry VI and rule as Edward IV. (Ian Downes)

35. Silver coin hoard (YORYM-62D744, 2005 T534)
Medieval, AD 1135–1153
Discovered in 2007 in 'York Area', East Riding and acquired by the Treasure House, Beverley.

This hoard contains five pennies, two cut halfpennies, and one fragment of a penny. Three of the complete pennies and both cut halves are bent. All the coins are of King Stephen (AD 1135–53) and date from AD 1136–1145.

The period of Stephen's rule is known as 'the Anarchy', as it was a time of political unrest and civil war. Stephen seized the throne on the death of his uncle, Henry I, despite having vowed to support Mathilda, Henry's daughter. Mathilda fought for her right to rule, and took control of south-west England, while Stephen controlled the south-east. During this turbulent period, many irregular coins were struck and also issued from dies that had been deliberately defaced, possibly as a rejection of Stephen's authority. This may also suggest why some of the coins in this hoard were bent.

Following years of war, Mathilda's son Henry and Stephen negotiated a peace, with Henry being named heir to the throne and eventually becoming Henry II.

YORYM-62D744 (2005 T534): A silver coin hoard from 'York Area', East Riding.

36. Silver seal matrix (YORYM-13A179, 2015 T472)
Medieval, AD 1200–1400
Discovered in 2015 in Markington, North Yorkshire.

This seal matrix would have been used to make an impression in wax to seal a document or authenticate a signature. It is set with a reused Roman intaglio, dating from the second to third centuries AD. The intaglio is made of a red stone, and is engraved with a winged Victory facing a seated male figure with a cockerel at his feet. This is likely to represent a winged messenger saluting the god Jupiter. The matrix itself bears a legend meaning 'Secret Messenger' suggesting the matrix was made to fit with the intaglio's design and that whoever made the seal understood the meaning of the intaglio.

Ancient gems were commonly reused in personal seal matrices throughout the Medieval period, particularly the twelfth to fourteenth centuries, and were often employed as privy or counter-seals by officials. It is unclear exactly how Roman intaglios came to be reused in such quantities, although it is possible that they were found locally by peasants working the land and passed to their lords. It is equally possible that they were imported specifically. The way in which intaglios were viewed and interpreted by medieval people shows the continuing impact of one civilisation on another.

YORYM-13A179 (2015 T472): A silver seal matrix from Markington, North Yorkshire.

37. Copper-alloy unfinished strap clasps (SWYOR-6B5350)
Medieval, AD 1250–1500
Discovered in 2012 in Naburn, York.

These two strap clasps are failed castings, still joined by the casting flashes that would normally be trimmed off the finished objects. It is unclear why they were not finished, as no serious flaws are apparent. Similar failed castings of buckles and strap slides have also been recovered from the neighbouring parish of Fulford.

Excavations in York have produced evidence for non-ferrous metalworking, particularly at the Bedern Foundry from AD 1250–1550, though the main products were cauldrons and other domestic vessels. A clay mould was found that may have been used for the large-scale production of small artefacts such as buckles. Miscast strap loops, buckles and strap ends were also recovered from the surrounding area. There was clearly manufacturing in the locality, though the exact location of the workshops is unknown.

Most failed castings would have been recycled in the next batch, but evidently some were missed. The examples recorded by the PAS were probably collected with rubbish, which was spread as fertiliser on fields in Naburn and Fulford, and are further evidence of the manufacture of small metal objects in York.

SWYOR-6B5350: Two copper-alloy unfinished strap clasps, made in a single casting, from Naburn, York.

A finished copper-alloy strap clasp from Brodsworth, Doncaster, showing what the failed castings SWYOR-6B5350 would have looked like if they had been completed (SWYOR-AC2642).

A copper-alloy pair of miscast or unfinished strap slides from Fulford, York (SWYOR-76F578).

38. Copper-alloy pilgrim badge (LVPL-6B1F98)
Medieval, AD 1400–1500
Discovered in 2012 in Skirpenbeck, East Riding.

This religious souvenir depicts St Roch in his characteristic pose of exposing a plague sore at his groin. Such souvenirs were purchased at shrines by pilgrims, who wore them to show they had completed their pilgrimage. They were also thought to hold magical properties that could prevent or cure illness.

St Roch is believed to have been born at Montpellier, where he is honoured. He tended sufferers of the plague in Italy, before succumbing to the disease himself. St Roch isolated himself and miraculously survived, thanks to a dog that brought him bread and licked his wounds, healing them. Upon his return to Montpellier, he was imprisoned after being falsely accused of being a spy, and later died in prison. He is invoked against sickness, particularly the plague, and is the patron saint of dogs and the falsely accused.

LVPL-6B1F98: A copper-alloy pilgrim badge, depicting St Roch from Skirpenbeck, East Riding.

39. Copper-alloy pyx lid (YORYM-58EB27)
Medieval, AD 1350–1400
Discovered in 2008 in Arncliffe, North Yorkshire.

Pyxes were used in Catholic masses as a container for the host – the communion bread that represents the body of Christ. A broken hinge remains on the lid, indicating that this one was in use for quite some time, and a loop opposite the hinge would have been used to lock the vessel, with a string or pin slotted through the hole to secure it.

This example has Limoges-style enamelled decoration (named after the French city in which the style developed) and is gilded. While Limoges style originated in twelfth-century France, British craftspeople were copying and developing the technique into the late thirteenth century.

The pyx lid was found with two fragments of a late medieval copper-alloy crown, probably from a wooden statue. They were probably deposited together, perhaps after a theft from a church or during the Reformation.

YORYM-58EB27: A copper-alloy pyx lid from Arncliffe, North Yorkshire.

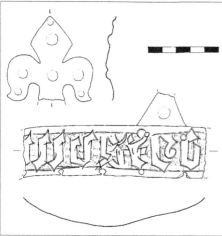

An illustration of the two copper-alloy crown fragments found with the Arncliffe pyx lid.

40. Silver-gilt livery badge (YORYM-1716A4, 2010 T471)
Medieval, AD 1483–1485
Discovered in 2010 in Stillingfleet, North Yorkshire and acquired by the Yorkshire Museum; YORYM:2012.577.

This silver-gilt livery badge is in the form of a boar facing left, with a loop for attachment remaining in the centre of the reverse. The white boar was a symbol of Richard III (AD 1483–1485), used by his household and followers. Richard distributed numerous boar badges, including 13,000 in cloth, at his coronation and at the installation of his son Edward as Prince of Wales.

Livery badges were important symbols of political affiliation, produced in lead, silver, and gilded copper, and could be worn pinned to the chest or a hat. Badges in precious metals would have been given to Richard's more important supporters.

YORYM-1716A4: A silver-gilt boar badge from Stillingfleet, York, used as an emblem of Richard III. (York Museums Trust (Yorkshire Museum) [CC By-SA 4.0] accession number YORYM:2012.577)

Chapter 5
Post-Medieval

Henry VII's defeat of Richard III at the Battle of Bosworth in AD 1485 marks the beginning of the Tudor dynasty and the Post-Medieval period.

Henry VII was of Lancastrian stock but, by marrying Elizabeth of York, Edward IV's daughter, he united the houses of Lancaster and York. They adopted the symbol of the Tudor rose, combining the red and white rose emblems of their houses. It was used on fashionable dress accessories of the time.

A significant event of the period was the Dissolution of the Monasteries by Henry VIII in AD 1536–1540. Feeling that monastic houses held too much power and wealth, Henry set about diverting some of these riches to the Crown, dividing and selling their assets to the aristocracy. As a consequence, around 120 religious institutions were closed or destroyed throughout Yorkshire.

The Dissolution allowed entrepreneurs to take over the profitable wool trade that had been largely controlled by monasteries. Kirkstall Abbey's land was sold, for example, allowing local people to farm sheep in Leeds; the wealth generated from this fueled its later expansion into a city. The wool industry is reflected in many objects found in Yorkshire, including shield-shaped weights used to weigh fleeces. As the system of taxing wool products became ever more complex, lead seals were attached to bales of cloth to show that the necessary taxes had been paid.

The reign of Elizabeth I, the last monarch of the Tudor dynasty, was a time of great prosperity. This was Shakespeare's age, in which arts and culture flowered. Great explorers such as Sir Francis Drake and Yorkshire's Sir Martin Frobisher explored the world, claiming overseas possessions and establishing trading posts. This was the start of the mighty British Empire, which reached its peak in the eighteenth century.

By the end of her reign, Elizabeth was a popular monarch. Many of her coins recorded by the PAS are especially worn, partly because of their long circulation, but also because, reputedly, her face was rubbed to evoke good luck.

Scotland and England were united into one country when Elizabeth left no heir and James Stuart of Scotland was asked to take the English throne. The extravagant lifestyle of Stuart kings caused disagreements with Parliament; tensions ran high and, under Charles I, the country descended into civil war. No longer safe in London, Charles relocated to York, and much of the fighting in AD 1642–1644 occurred in Yorkshire.

The Parliamentarians allied with Scottish forces, shifting the balance of power, and, in AD 1644, they defeated the Royalists at the Battle of Marston Moor – reputedly the largest battle ever fought in Britain, although it lasted only two hours. The civil wars continued until a Parliamentary victory in AD 1651.

A copper-alloy dress hook (clothing fastener), decorated with a Tudor rose, which became a fashionable symbol of the period (YORYM-EC41D9).

A lead-alloy cloth seal from Aston cum Aughton, Rotherham. It appears to depict a sheep and, since a hanging sheep or the golden fleece is one of the symbols of Leeds, it seems likely that this seal was associated with a company or individual involved in the cloth trade in Leeds (SWYOR-DC9677).

A silver threepence coin of Elizabeth I from Bentley, Doncaster, showing how her face has been rubbed smooth (SWYOR-7F1CC8).

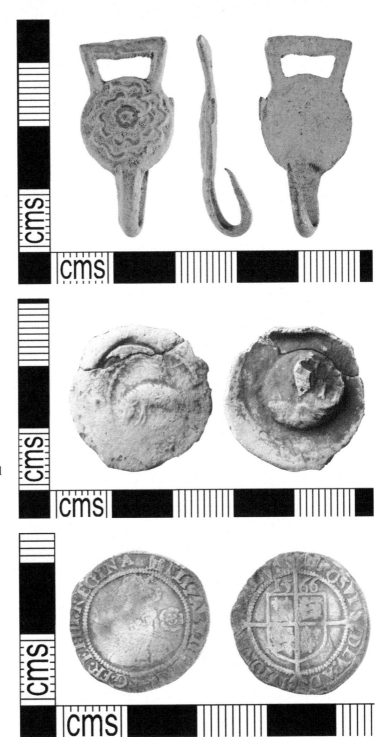

In January AD 1649, Charles was tried, convicted, and executed for high treason. The monarchy was abolished, and the republic Commonwealth of England was declared, but the population soon tired of Cromwell's strict Puritan rules. Eventually, Charles II was restored to the throne in AD 1660. The Church of England was reinstated, theatres reopened, and people reportedly 'pranced around maypoles as a way of taunting the Presbyterians and Independents' (Harris, 2005).

While North and East Yorkshire retained a broadly rural economy with pockets of industry, during the later Post-Medieval period South and West Yorkshire's landscape changed markedly, as mining, metalworking, weaving, and tanning became the main areas of employment.

Sheffield became the main centre of cutlery production in England and was the leading supplier worldwide, becoming known as 'the City of Steel' when it expanded its metalworking specialism. The Yorkshire wool industry also continued to thrive, and Wakefield became the most important wool marketing centre. Large cloth marketing halls, such as Halifax's Piece Hall, were built to showcase the wares of hundreds of local manufacturers. The rapid growth of industrial cities created unsanitary conditions, inspiring some mill-owners to build model villages for their workers. One prime example is Saltaire, Bradford.

Industrial processes increased the demand for coal. More mines were needed, and the canal network was developed (later to be replaced by railways) to ease the transportation of coal and other goods. These developments moulded the modern industrial landscape and infrastructure that we see today.

The Industrial Revolution of the late eighteenth and early nineteenth centuries saw increased mechanisation and mass-production. Consequently, the PAS is selective in recording finds from this period and generally focuses on those artefacts that are of particular historical or social interest.

Some of the ruins of Pontefract Castle, Wakefield. It was described by Cromwell as England's strongest inland garrison. Many of Yorkshire's castles, such as Helmsley and Pontefract, were deliberately dismantled by the townspeople after the Civil Wars to prevent them being refortified and bringing further disruption to the town should any more fighting occur.

A seventeenth-century powder measure cap from Castleford Central and Glasshoughton, Wakefield, only a few miles from Pontefract Castle. Every musketeer in the Civil Wars wore a bandolier fitted with twelve powder measures, each containing the powder for a single shot. The caps from the measures are common finds recorded with the PAS (SWYOR-8067D6).

A silver Commonwealth shilling from Thornton-Le-Dale, North Yorkshire, showing the arms of the Commonwealth – the conjoined shields of St George and Ireland (YORYM-7182D4).

The courtyard of the Halifax Piece Hall, as depicted in an oil painting by J. W. Anderson, held in the Calderdale Museums collection. This building was described with pride by Thompson in *A Brief Guide to the Industrial Heritage of West Yorkshire* as 'perhaps the finest monument to the domestic textile industry in the world'! (Calderdale MBC Museums)

Salts Mill at Saltaire, Bradford, was built in the 1850s when businessman and philanthropist Sir Titus Salt relocated and expanded his woollen mills on a new site on the edge of the city, and constructed an accompanying model community to house his workers. The whole village is now a UNESCO site.

41. Silver knotted coin (SWYOR-12B278)
Post-Medieval, AD 1547–1553
Discovered in 2015 in Hickleton, Doncaster.

This silver coin of Edward VI has been cut into two pieces, with the centre removed, and then loosely folded, leaving the denomination and issue unidentifiable. The reasons for this treatment are unclear. The knot may have been intentional, or the pieces may simply be waste after cutting out the central part of the coin.

Pilgrimage records describe an 'English custom' of bending coins when evoking a saint to cure an illness or affliction. A silver coin was bent over the sufferer, pledging it to the saint. The pilgrim would take the folded coin to the relevant shrine, hoping for miraculous relief.

Some of the hundreds of deliberately damaged coins recorded with the PAS may be the result of this custom. Some were deliberately placed in fields to bless them – the coin having absorbed religious power from its pilgrimage. Pilgrim souvenirs were also used in this way. Other mutilated coins were probably bound to the patient and then lost accidentally.

Though we can't be certain, it is possible that this knotted coin was bent as part of a similar ritual. Interestingly, its treatment seems to be more elaborate than simple folding.

Right: SWYOR-12B278: A silver mutilated coin from Hickleton, Doncaster.

Below: A coin that was bent double when found, from Fulford, York. A fragment of textile was found surviving inside, perhaps part of the cloth that was used to bind it in place on an ailment (SWYOR-4F7776).

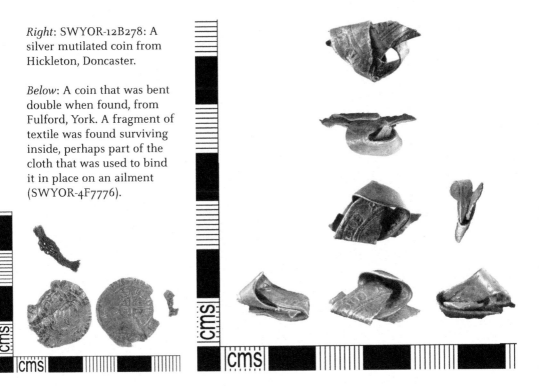

81

42. Silver and gold coin hoard (SWYOR-FDBB70, 2011 T 428)
Post-Medieval, AD 1645–1646
Discovered in 2011 in Ackworth, Wakefield and acquired by Pontefract Museum.

While levelling his garden, an Ackworth resident disturbed a buried pot and watched in astonishment as gold and silver coins cascaded out of it 'like a slot machine'. 591 coins were recovered, including fifty-two of gold, along with a finger ring inscribed, 'when this you see remember me'.

The latest coins date from AD 1645–1646, in the middle of the English Civil Wars, suggesting the hoard was buried then. During these years, the nearby Pontefract Castle was besieged twice by the Parliamentarians, some of whom were housed in Ackworth.

When buried, the hoard was worth £85 12s 0d, making it one of the larger Civil Wars hoards known. Hoards are usually savings or emergency caches, wherein the owner has hidden whatever valuables they had at a time of threat, as in this case. Barclay and Besley explain that, 'In an age without banks, every town and village would, at any given time, be the hiding place for numerous hoards. In times of war or unrest, the chances of an individual being unable to recover their valuables through death or displacement were much increased'.

Twelve of the coins are *ducatons* from the Spanish Netherlands. These have an interesting story of their own, as they are often found in Yorkshire Civil Wars hoards. Queen Henrietta Maria sailed for Europe in AD 1642 to raise funds for the war. She sent a 'little barrel of ducatoons' back and carried more with her when she returned in AD 1643. She landed in Bridlington and travelled south across Yorkshire. Research by Besley has

SWYOR-FDBB70 (2011 T428): The vessel, finger ring and some of the coins from the Ackworth Hoard from Ackworth, Wakefield, on display in Pontefract Museum. (Photographed with the kind permission of Wakefield Council)

shown that the findspots of *ducatons* closely follow the Queen's route, suggesting she used the money raised abroad to pay her way. This route included a stay in Pontefract in March AD 1643, and the coins distributed then probably circulated locally or were saved for a few years until entering this hoard.

The gold posy finger ring from the Ackworth Hoard with its sentimental internal inscription: 'when this you see remember me'.

The coins were initially sorted at the finder's house to establish the number and chronology.

A large silver *ducaton* of Albert and Elizabeth of the Spanish Netherlands, one of the twelve *ducatons* found in the hoard; they were probably distributed by Queen Henrietta Maria in AD 1643.

43. Copper-alloy trade token (YORYM-0EE3C7)
Post-Medieval, AD 1666
Discovered in 2015 in Boroughbridge, North Yorkshire.

Trade tokens were issued in AD 1648–1673, at a time when there was little low-denomination coinage issued by the Crown. In response, traders and business proprietors began producing tokens to be used within their local area.

A variety of information was given on tokens, including the place of issue, the issuer's name, their trade, and the denomination. This example is a halfpenny token issued by John Preston, a grocer in Bradford, and is dated AD 1666. Trade tokens rarely travel far from their place of issue and, as such, provide a wonderful insight into the trade of the time.

On 16 August AD 1672, a proclamation by the Crown ordered the minting of trade tokens to cease. This was largely ignored and two further proclamations were issued in subsequent years, the latter finally being effective.

Above: YORYM-0EE3C7: A copper-alloy trade token from Boroughbridge, North Yorkshire.

Left: A similar trade token found in Stainforth, North Yorkshire, names William Taylor, a draper in Settle. This token was donated to the Museum of North Craven Life, Settle, by the finder (SWYOR-5C8D60).

84

44. Lead toy hornbook (YORYM-FA8FF1)
Post-Medieval, AD 1670
Found in 2013 in Market Weighton.

Increased literacy in the Post-Medieval period led to the creation of teaching aids such as hornbooks. Real hornbooks were large tablets, printed with the text to be learnt – usually the Lord's Prayer or the alphabet. They were commonly made of wood, onto which the printed paper was mounted and covered with a thin sheet of transparent cow horn for protection.

Small lead versions like this one are mass-produced copies. They often have errors, making them unhelpful for teaching, and so it has been suggested that they are toys that mimic hornbooks for children in poorer or less-educated families, or even that they were hornbooks owned by dolls.

Mistakes on this example include the 'N' and 'S' being reversed. 'J' and 'U' are missing because they were not used in the seventeenth-century alphabet. The reverse inscription means, 'Thomas of other good art made me. 1670', but is oddly produced in a mixture of English and Latin. It is unusual to have any text on the reverse of toy hornbooks.

YORYM-FA8FF1: A lead toy hornbook from Market Weighton, East Riding.

45. Lead-alloy cloth seal (YORYM-0C7954)
Post-Medieval, AD 1500–1650
Discovered in 2014 in Cottingwith, East Riding.

Lead cloth seals were used in Europe to mark cloth for commercial sale between the thirteenth and nineteenth centuries, and were part of a system of regulation and quality control. In England, seals were added by the maker – the weaver or clothier – and the regulating authority to show that the quality of the product was good enough for market. They also indicated that tax on the production of textiles had been paid to the Crown. Cloth seals typically comprise two discs joined by a strip, which were folded around the textile and stamped closed.

These seals provide a great deal of information about the import and export of textiles. This example bears the letter 'A' on the obverse, while the reverse depicts a pinecone. These symbols indicate that the seal originated in Augsburg, Germany, as the pinecone is the heraldic badge of the city. Such seals were attached to fustians and Haarlem textiles – varieties of heavy cloth woven from cotton and chiefly prepared for menswear. Other cloth seals found in Yorkshire indicate cloth from different places of origin.

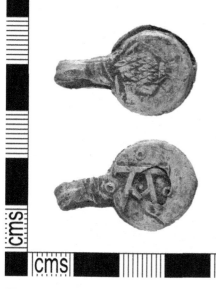

YORYM-0C7954: A lead-alloy cloth seal from Cottingwith, East Riding.

A lead-alloy London cloth seal from Kellington, North Yorkshire. The seventeenth-century seal depicts an angel, which was used to identify cloth from London (SWYOR-F71605).

46. Silver pendant (SWYOR-817B56, 2013 T35)
Post-Medieval, AD 1600–1700
Discovered in 2013 in Raskelf, North Yorkshire.

This silver locket would have been worn, probably secretly, by a faithful Catholic during a time of religious persecution. The pendant evokes Jesus and Mary, and has an unusual construction, with a screw in the base sealing the lid shut. The chamber was designed to hold a small relic – in this example, a piece of bone.

There are other very similar examples recorded with the PAS; these are from North Yorkshire and Leeds, with two from one field in Northumberland. These pendants are thought to have been made in Europe, so it is interesting to wonder how they came to northern England. Concentrations in particular locations may indicate places where people gathered to worship secretly or the presence of foreign Catholics.

SWYOR-817B56 (2013 T35): A silver pendant locket with a fragment of bone found inside, from Raskelf, North Yorkshire.

A matching locket found in Leeds (SWYOR-4BFBAD). In addition, SWYOR-9D6547 was found in North Yorkshire and two other examples were found in one field in Northumberland: DUR-3B7822 and NCL-912218. They are all of very similar design.

87

47. Copper-alloy nocturnal (LVPL-25A4C7)
Medieval to Post-Medieval, AD 1300–1650
Discovered in 2012 in Kellington, North Yorkshire.

The Age of Enlightenment saw the increased use of scientific instruments. This nocturnal would have been used for telling the time at night, although only fragments of this example survive. The letters on the dial are the initial letters of months. The dial has been deliberately cut rather than broken, perhaps suggesting that the object was dismantled intentionally.

To use the nocturnal, the index marker is set to the current date on the dial face. The pole star is viewed through the central hole, and the alidade (a moveable marker that projects beyond the face) is lined up to the star for which the instrument is designed. Several stars, which rotate around the pole star, can be used to calculate time. The time can then be read off another smaller dial, and is indicated by the edge of the alidade.

The earliest historical reference to a nocturnal is in a twelfth-century manuscript, but most of the instruments known today date from the sixteenth century onwards. There are only seven possible nocturnals recorded with the PAS.

LVPL-25A4C7: A fragmentary copper-alloy nocturnal (a scientific instrument for telling the time at night), found in Kellington, North Yorkshire.

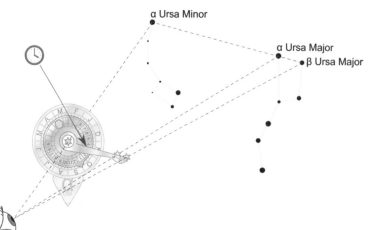

A diagram showing a complete Post-Medieval nocturnal and the way it functioned. (Johann 'nojhan' Dréo — CC-BY-SA [CC BY-SA 3.0], https://upload. wikimedia. org/wikipedia/ commons/3/3c/ Nocturnal_howto. svg)

48. Silver hawking vervel (YORYM-7576F7, 2012 T579)
Post-Medieval, AD 1600–1700
Discovered in 2012 in Sutton-Upon-Derwent, East Riding.

Hawking has been a favourite form of hunting for centuries in England and was at its most popular in the seventeenth century. It is the pastime of using a trained bird of prey to catch animals such as hares. As these birds were prestigious and expensive, their owners fitted them with vervels – small rings attached to their leg straps. Vervels gave the owner's name, residence or coat of arms, allowing lost birds to be identified and returned. Arms were especially useful, as not everyone could read.

Examples made of silver illustrate the development of hawking as an aristocratic pastime in the seventeenth century. This vervel is inscribed with the name '*F. VAGHAN' and has a shield-shaped plate, bearing the crest of a male head with a snake wrapped around his throat. This crest is attributed to the Vaughn family of East Yorkshire, Herefordshire and Wales. While this object was found in East Yorkshire, the Herefordshire branch of the Vaughn family were based at Hergest Court, which was allegedly the inspiration for Sir Arthur Conan Doyle's Sherlock Holmes adventure *The Hound of the Baskervilles*.

Right: A peregrine falcon, a bird used for hawking, perched on the falconer's hand. The jesses (the leather straps attached to the bird's legs) are just visible. Vervels would have been attached to these. (Chris Downes)

Below: YORYM-7576F7 (2012 T579): A silver hawking vervel from Sutton-Upon-Derwent, East Riding.

49. Gold posy ring (YORYM-C2732F, 2016 T208)
Post-Medieval, AD 1500–1700
Discovered in 2016 in Brantingham, East Riding.

Finger rings bearing inscriptions are referred to as 'posy' rings, from the French '*poésie*' or poetry. The inscription is generally found on the interior of the ring, hidden to everyone except the wearer. This ring is inscribed internally with sentimental text reading, 'I LYKE MI CHOVS TO WEL TO CHANG' ('I Like My Choice Too Well to Change').

The practice of giving rings engraved with mottoes at betrothals or weddings was common in England from the sixteenth century onwards, and continued until the late eighteenth century. Posy rings could also be given on other occasions as a token of friendship or loyalty, and could contain religious or memorial inscriptions. Most of the sentimental mottoes were taken from popular literature of the time.

YORYM-C2732F (2016 T208): A gold posy finger ring from Brantringham, East Riding.

50. Lead flax bale seal (YORYM-963949)
Post-Medieval, AD 1776
Discovered in 2015 in Welton, East Riding.

Although it is less than 300 years old, this flax seal was recorded by the PAS because it displays information allowing named individuals to be identified. Bale seals are good evidence for Britain's textile trade with Russia, which was one of the main exporters of flax for making sailcloth, rope, webbing and linen in the eighteenth and nineteenth centuries.

Bale seals were part of a system of regulation and quality control, and were applied individually by a port inspector. They record the inspector's name, the post at which they worked, and the quality and grade of the flax, as well as the date and the name of the port.

The letters 'NP' on this example indicate that the bale was shipped from Narva, Estonia, in the Baltic States. The Cyrillic lettering on the obverse identifies the officer for flax inspection as 'L'nyanoy Dosmotr' and the other lines name the quality-control officer as 'T. Chupyatov'.

The findspots of Russian bale seals often correspond with the location of flax mills, though this one may be related to the nearby ports of Hull and Goole. The flax industry was important in the East Riding with flax mills nearby in Gilberdyke and Howden, as well as other parts of the county.

YORYM-963949: A Russian lead flax bale seal from Welton, East Riding.

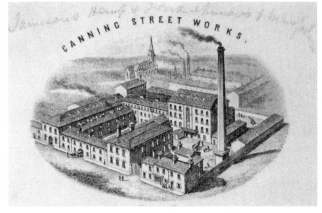

A Canning Street Flax Mill trade card, depicting one of the flax mills in the East Riding. (Hull and East Riding Museum, Hull Museums accession number KINCM:2007.5509 – Wilberforce House)

Conclusion

Yorkshire is a huge geographical area. It is the biggest county in Britain, and one that is key to the history of the nation. When recovered from the ground and recorded with the PAS, objects left behind by our ancestors can reveal Yorkshire's hidden history. The fifty finds showcased here were selected to tell as many different stories from diverse eras and varied landscapes as possible.

Artefacts recorded with the PAS are many and varied, and their distribution is of great importance to archaeologists and the public alike, allowing everyone to better understand the landscape, as well as how people lived and worked in the past. With such a diverse range of material, and over 57,000 objects from which to choose, it was very difficult to select just fifty that best represent the wealth of information offered by the archaeology of Yorkshire.

Some of the finds were chosen because they are spectacular and unmissable highlights. Others are more mundane, but illustrate important aspects of life in the past, such as trade or manufacture. Others we liked because they were unusual or quirky, but each object helps to give a sense of the huge range of material that we, as FLOs, are lucky enough to work with every day.

Left: A view along Wharfdale from Ilkley Moor, Bradford.

Right: A Yorkshire farmhouse and barn near Fewston, Harrogate. (Jack Coulthard)

By systematically recording finds, no matter how poorly preserved, common, or incomplete they are, we can learn more about our shared past. The accurate recording of precise findspots for each and every object can sharpen the focus of our research. Advances in GPS technology, smartphones and mapping software mean that finders are able to record more easily and accurately than ever before. We celebrate that, in 2015, all finds recorded by the North and East Yorkshire FLO had a six-figure National Grid Reference (NGR) or better. This identifies 100 metres squared, and is the minimum level of detail that can still be of use to researchers; however, 53 per cent of those finds had a much more accurate ten- or twelve-figure NGR. Over 70 per cent of the finds recorded by the South and West Yorkshire FLO had an eight-figure NGR or better. On the database, we only publicise findspots to a four-figure NGR to respect the privacy of finders and landowners, and to protect sites from criminal activity. Exact findspots are available to authorised researchers who adhere to the PAS's confidentiality procedures.

An important feature of the PAS is the recording of unusual and rare objects. Some of the objects in this book are unique or scarce in the archaeological record, and recording them helps with the interpretation of objects that were previously poorly understood.

Searching for and recording finds with the PAS can save artefacts from destruction. Arable farming practices can be harmful to archaeological deposits, but retrieving objects that have already been disturbed, and recording as much information about them as possible, helps to mitigate this damage. Archaeology that is buried where it is not under immediate threat, such as pasture land, is best left undisturbed, as digging can disturb

A freshly unearthed Medieval thimble.

An arable landscape in North Yorkshire. (Ian Downes)

layers of stratified archaeology, causing damage and loss of information. For this reason, the PAS does not encourage metal detecting on undisturbed pasture, and suggests that archaeology below the plough zone should not be disturbed.

Recording objects with the PAS is a way for local communities to engage with their heritage. Not only can finders contribute directly to our knowledge through recording, but the objects are also available online for use by schoolchildren and individuals interested in tracing the history of their local area. The PAS also allows people to enhance local knowledge by recording objects discovered by chance in gardens and allotments, eroded from footpaths or unearthed by moles.

The extensive archaeology of Yorkshire has encouraged many local history societies, archaeology groups and metal-detecting clubs to flourish. The members of these varied groups are all bound by their shared passion for the county's fascinating past. The PAS is a rich source of data, and talks given by FLOs to these groups help to further engage communities with local archaeology.

History tends to be the story of royalty and powerful people, and less of everyday life and the lower classes. Objects recorded by the PAS can redress the balance by fleshing out written sources with real, sometimes humble, objects that were used and lost by our ancestors. We rejoice in the diligence of responsible finders, who discover and declare such finds with excellent findspot information. It is through their discoveries that we can better understand the history of individual places, and catch a glimpse of the normal people of the past, the people like us. As finders and FLOs, it is a privilege to unearth, study and record these artefacts and, in the process, to hold history in our hands.

Left: Rebecca Griffiths discussing finds at a talk to a local society.

Right: Amy Downes recording a Roman trumpet brooch onto the PAS database.

Further Reading and Bibliography

Allason-Jones, L. and Miket, R. F., *Catalogue of Small Finds from South Shields Roman Fort* (Gloucester: Society of Antiquaries of London, 1984).

Barclay, C. and Besly, E., *A Little Barrel of Ducatoons: The Civil War Coinage of Yorkshire* (York: Yorkshire Museum, 1994).

Becker, K., *Iron Age Ring-Headed Pins in Ireland and Britain and on the Continent* (Mainz: Verlag des R., 2008).

Birley, E., *Roman Bronze Arm-Purses* (Newcastle: Archaeologia Aeliana, 1963).

Bishop, M. C., 'Military Equipment' in Cool, H. E. M., and Philo, C. (eds), *Roman Castleford Volume 1* (Exeter: West Yorkshire Archaeology Service, 1998).

Cool, H. E. M., *Made in Castleford* (Unpublished, 2010).

Cool, H. E. M. and Philo, C., *Roman Castleford Volume 1* (Exeter: West Yorkshire Archaeology Service, 1998).

Cool, H. E. M., *Romano-British Bracelets and Bangles* (Barbican Research Associates) Consulted at www.barbicanra.co.uk/resources.html, 2016.

East Riding of Yorkshire Council and Carl Bro and Golder Associates, *EAST RIDING OF YORKSHIRE LANDSCAPE CHARACTER ASSESSMENT* (East Riding of Yorkshire: East Riding of Yorkshire Council, 2005). Consulted at www2.eastriding.gov.uk/environment/planning-and-building-control/east-riding-local-plan/landscape-character-assessment.

Egan, G., *Material Culture in London in an Age of Transition: Tudor and Stuart Period Finds c. 1450–c. 1700 from Excavations at Riverside Sites in Southwark.* (London: MoLAS Monograph 19, 2005).

Geake, H., *When Were Hanging Bowls Deposited in Anglo-Saxon Graves?* (Leeds: Maney and Son, 1999).

Gomersall, H., *West Yorkshire Archaeology Advisory Service Research Agenda: Industrial Archaeology* (Wakefield: West Yorkshire Archaeology Advisory Service, 2005). Consulted at www.wyjs.org.uk. Green, M. J., *The Gods of Roman Britain* (Aylesbury: Shire Publications, 1983).

Harris, Tim, *Restoration: Charles II and His Kingdoms 1660–1685* (London: Allen Lane, 2005).

Hattatt, R., *Ancient and Romano-British Brooches* (Sherborne: Dorset Publishing, 1982).

Henig, M., *Religion in Roman Britain* (London: B. T. Batsford, 1984).

Jackson, R., *Cosmetic Sets of Late Iron Age and Roman Britain* (London: British Museum Research Publication number 181, 2010).

Johns, C., *The Jewellery of Roman Britain* (London: UCL Press, 1996).

Kelleher, R., 'The "English Custom"; bent coins in Medieval England' in *Treasure Hunting, April Issue 2010* (Essex: ACG Publications Ltd, 2010).

Lewis, M., 'Leaden dolls, books and seals' in Harnow, H. *et al* (eds), *Across the North Sea: Later Historical Archaeology in Britain and Denmark,*. c. *1500–2000 AD* (Copenhagan: University Press of Southern Denmark, 2012).

Moorhead, S., *A History of Roman Coinage in Britain* (Essex: Green Light Publishing, 2013).

Moorhead, S., 'A Survey of Roman coin finds from Hertfordshire' in Lockyear, K. (ed), *Archaeology in Hertfordshire: Recent Research* (Hertfordshire: University of Hertfordshire Press, 2013).

Naylor, J. and Allen, M., 'A new variety of gold shilling of the "York" group' in Abramson, T. (ed), *Studies in Early Medieval Coinage: Sifting the Evidence* (London: Spink and Son Ltd, 2014).

Ottaway, P., *Roman Yorkshire: People, Culture and Landscape* (Pickering: Blackthorn Press, 2013).

Ottaway, P. and Rogers, N. (eds), *Craft, Industry and Everyday Life: Finds from Medieval York. The Archaeology of York, The Small Finds, fascicule 17/15* (York: York Archaeological Trust, 2002).

Portable Antiquities Scheme, *Portable Antiquities and Treasure Annual Report 2007* (London: British Museum Press, 2009).

Simmons, I. G. *et al*, 'Prehistoric Environments' in Spratt, D. A. (ed.), *Prehistoric and Roman Archaeology of North-East Yorkshire* (London: Council for British Archaeology, 1993).

Spratt, D. A., *Prehistoric and Roman Archaeology of North-East Yorkshire* (London: Council for British Archaeology, 1999).

Thompson, W. J. (ed.), *A Brief Guide to the Industrial Heritage of West Yorkshire* (Ironbridge, Telford: Association for Industrial Archaeology, 1989).

Wagemans, G. M. C., *The Roman Pentagon Dodecahedron. An Astronomic Measuring Instrument.* (Consulted at http://www.dodecaeder.nl/en/hypothese, no date.)

Walton, P. J., *Rethinking Roman Britain: Coinage and Archaeology* (Belgium: Moneta, 2012).

Walton Rogers, P. and Riddler, I., 'Early Anglo-Saxon textile manufacturing implements from Saltwood Tunnel, Kent' in *Channel Tunnel Rail Link, London and Continental Railways. Oxford Wessex Archaeology Joint Venture. London and Continental Railways.* (CTRL Specialist Report Series, 2006). Consulted at http://archaeologydataservice.ac.uk.

Worrell, S., 'Finds Reported under the Portable Antiquities Scheme' in *Britannia Volume XXXIX* (London: Cambridge University Press, 2008).